The Great Wines of France

Penn & Sally:
Christmas 2005.
All thé Best!

CLIVE COATES MW

The Great Wines of France

FRANCE'S TOP DOMAINES AND THEIR WINES

MITCHELL BEAZLEY

The Great Wines of France
by Clive Coates MW

First published in Great Britain in 2005 by Mitchell Beazley, an imprint of
Octopus Publishing Group Ltd, 2–4 Heron Quays, London E14 4JP

Copyright © Octopus Publishing Group Ltd 2005
Text copyright © Clive Coates MW 2005

A CIP record for this book is available from the British Library

Set in Nofret

Printed and bound in China by Toppan Printing Company Limited

ISBN 1 84000 992 6

Commissioning Editor: Hilary Lumsden
Executive Art Editor: Yasia Williams
Managing Editor: Juanne Branquinho
Editor: Susanna Forbes
Picture Research: Emma O'Neill, Juanne Branquinho
Index: Hilary Bird
Production: Gary Hayes

Contents

Introduction

How do you define a *great* wine — as opposed to one which is merely very good and highly satisfying? I would define it thus: a great wine, the moment you savour it, offers you a glimpse of perfection. Like a great piece of music or a great painting, there is an element of certainty: you feel it could not be any better.

Wine is the product of the earth. In a few parts of the world the combination of geology, microclimate, aspect, and drainage — what wine people call terroir — plus the correct choice of grape variety and the perfectionism of an intelligent winemaker open up the possibility, if the weather conditions in the run-up to the vintage are auspicious, of great wine.

Great wines please the intellect as much as the palate. Wines which are the product of a slow gestation — a long season between bud-break and harvest as well as a long period between fermentation and maturity — are inevitably more complex than their opposites. Great wines combine multi-dimensionality with depth and harmony. They have unmistakable originality. They speak of their origins. Above all, what they possess, lacking in lesser wines, is elegance and finesse, otherwise summarized by the word "breed".

This book is the product of a forty-year love affair with the fine wines of France. I am an unreconstructed Francophile. I would contend that France contains more great terroirs than any other wine-producing country. It is also home to most of the world's finest grape varieties. Moreover, most of its major wine areas — particularly

Bordeaux and Burgundy — lie at absolutely the right point of latitude, that warm temperate zone where the weather is neither too hot and dry, nor too cold and humid. Great wine, if the conditions are favourable, can be made here. It is also the wine country I know best.

The selection of estates featured in the pages which follow is, of course, a personal one. In the vast majority of cases, the properties are long-standing. I have been visiting them on a regular basis for the best part of forty years; the individuals behind the labels are good friends; and I have regularly been able to make comprehensive tastings of their wines. These domaines have a proven track record. They consistently produce brilliant wine. That is another facet of being "great".

In each case my profile of the property and those responsible for the wines is supplemented by notes on a dozen or so of their latest vintages. You will find these in the second part of the book. Some of these tastings were set up at my direct behest and took place *sur place*. Most of the top bordeaux were sampled at a series of First Growth tastings organized by the Institute of Masters of Wine. The bottles in these cases came direct from the properties themselves. In London, I have organized a series of my own Master tastings over the past few years. Others still were coordinated by friends. I would like to express my heartfelt thanks to all the individuals involved.

Last, but not least, as always, I must thank my personal assistant, Sonia Portalès. I would be lost without you!

bordeaux

Bordeaux produces the most profound, the most noble, and the most intellectually challenging wines in the world, especially if they are based on the Cabernet Sauvignon grape variety.

Ausone

BORDEAUX

AUSONE IS TRIPLY UNIQUE IN BORDEAUX: OF ALL THE TOP ESTATES
IT IS THE SMALLEST, IT IS THE ONLY ONE ON A SLOPE, AND IT IS
THE SOLE GRAND PROPERTY BASED ON LIMESTONE ROCK.

CHÂTEAU AUSONE

SAINT·ÉMILION
1ᵉʳ GRAND CRU CLASSÉ "A"

→ 2001 ←

FAMILLE VAUTHIER
Propriétaire

OPPOSITE *The thirteenth-century*
Chapelle Madelaine

If one approaches St-Emilion from the south from the long straight road which connects Libourne with Castillon, one will drive between Château Canon-La-Gaffelière — the *chais* on the left, the château on the right — and then up a slender valley towards the narrow cobbled streets of the town itself.

On the steep slopes up on the left is a small vineyard whose aspect is south and east. There are the seven hectares of Château Ausone. Behind the château of Ausone are further vineyards on the plateau itself which belong to neighbouring Belair. In one of these fields, now hidden behind clumps of bramble and broom, are some ancient ruins. These show clearly how the vine was cultivated from the time of the Roman poet Ausonius right up until the early eighteenth century.

This ancient method was to plant the vines in a straight-line trench cut out of the local rock, here only a few centimetres below the surface. The sides of the trench were protected by stones, these being excavated from the local limestone caves, thus enlarging them into useful caverns within which the wine could be stored. Whether the vines at St-Emilion were grown alone or together with, say, fruit trees, up the branches of which the vine-canes could grow, and whether the vines were trained low or high on a pergola system is difficult to establish. The Romans had a number of techniques and these were exported and adapted throughout their Empire and over the centuries.

While there is plenty of other archaeological evidence of Gallo-Roman vineyard cultivation in the St-Emilion area, there is little in the way of documentary records to link people with places. What could be more natural than for the local inhabitants to "adopt" the poet Ausonius, known to have had several vineyards; and further that he should be identified specifically with one of the senior vineyards and one with a Roman ruin in its back garden?

The modern history of Ausone begins in the late nineteenth century with Edouard Dubois, who married the heiress to Ausone, Mademoiselle Challon, in 1891, having been manager of the estate for a number of years. He bought the neighbouring Château Belair in 1916 and died five years later in 1921.

ABOVE *The vineyard of Château*
Ausone in summer and winter

A century on, ownership was shared between Heylette Dubois-Challon, widow of Edouard's son – she passed away in 2003 – and her cousins, the Vauthier family. Madame Dubois-Challon, already owner of Belair in her own right, conceded her share of the control of Ausone in 1995, since when it has been managed by Alain Vauthier. Following Vauthier's arrival, considerable changes have taken place, including the construction of a new winery, and the wine now fully justifies its classification as one of only two *premier grand cru classé A* properties.

The vineyard, now protected against erosion and sudden bouts of excessive rain, comprises just over seven hectares, making it the smallest of all the top Bordeaux estates (it is also the only leading estate with vineyards on limestone soil and the only one on a slope - triply unique), and is planted with forty-five per cent Merlot and fifty-five per cent Cabernet Franc. The slope faces southeast and is protected from the cold north wind and westerly rain.

One of the features of Château Ausone was its splendid, extensive but regrettably rather damp natural cellar, a cavern in the rock behind the château and under the ruins of the thirteenth-century Chapelle Madelaine. The cellar has now been dried out, but is nevertheless no longer used the whole year round for barrel storage.

The wine is now made in a brand new *cuverie*, constructed in 2004 and 2005. Vinification takes place in small wooden vats, at a temperature of less than 30°C (86°F) at first, later being raised to a maximum of 32°C (90°F). There is now a second wine: La Chapelle d'Ausone.

Ausone in pre-Vauthier days was often promising when young, only to fail to live up to expectations ten years down the line. Today it is richer, fuller, firmer, and more concentrated, without having lost its inherent finesse. The 2003 is clearly the best wine of the Libournais.

Cheval-Blanc

BORDEAUX

THE VINEYARD OF CHATEAU CHEVAL-BLANC LIES ON THE WESTERN END
OF THE ST-EMILION REGION, CLOSER TO THE GREAT PROPERTIES OF
POMEROL THAN TO THE TOWN OF ST-EMILION ITSELF.

Cheval-Blanc lies in the smaller, more westerly, and more open terrain of the two parts of
the St-Emilion *vignoble*. Almost on the border with Pomerol, and in more gently undulating
country than round the village itself, is the Graves St-Emilion zone. The soil here, as the
name would suggest, contains gravel. Indeed it is a complex mixture of gravel, clay, and sand,
with pockets of limestone over a bed of hard iron rock, known as *crasse de fer*.

The earliest records show two *"maisons nobles"* in what is now the Graves St-Emilion: one at
Figeac, whose lands extended over Cheval-Blanc, and the other at Corbin, to the north. In two
stages, in 1832 and 1838, the Cheval-Blanc section was detached from the owners of Figeac
and was acquired by a family called Ducasse. Meanwhile the Fourcaud family, originally from
Lugon in the Dordogne, also owned vineyards in the area. In 1852, Jean Laussac Fourcaud
married Mademoiselle Henriette Ducasse. She brought as her dowry a property known as
Cheval-Blanc, at that time slightly more than thirty-one hectares and producing between
twenty-five and thirty *tonneaux* — casks — of wine. Not all of her estate was under vine.

At the time of the Fourcaud—Ducasse marriage the wines of the Graves St-Emilion (and,
similarly, those of Pomerol) were reckoned to be second class. All the *premiers crus* of
St-Emilion were on the *côtes*, headed by Belair. The senior Graves property was Figeac.

Jean Laussac Fourcaud set about buying up adjoining parcels of land and converting
suitable sections of it to vineyard. He was the first agriculturalist in St-Emilion to install a
proper system of drainage in his land. The vineyard expanded, production grew, and prices
gradually rose to equal the best of the St-Emilion *côtes*.

In 1893, Jean Laussac Fourcaud died, and was succeeded by Albert, one of his eight
children. He bought out the rest of the family and changed his name to Fourcaud-Laussac.
Albert himself had five children, and, before he died in 1927, made over Cheval-Blanc to a
Société Civile, a limited company owned by his children.

Up to 1989 Cheval-Blanc was managed by the genial Jacques Hébrard, husband of a
granddaughter of Albert. When he retired the direction passed into the hands of three ladies:
Claude de la Barre, Brigitte Hamelle, and Martine D'Arfeuille, all granddaughters of the

ABOVE *The avenue which leads
up to the château*

LEFT *The first-year barrel cellar
at Château Cheval-Blanc. After
twelve months the wine is moved
into the second-year barrel cellar*

Fourcaud-Laussacs. Pierre Lurton, formerly of Clos Fourtet, was appointed estate manager or *régisseur* in 1991. In 1998, after 150 years of Fourcaud-Laussac ownership, the family sold Château Cheval-Blanc to two millionaires: Bernard Arnault, chief executive of LVMH, and the Belgian businessman Albert Frère.

Lurton, a member of a many-tentacled vinous family, remembers a little difficulty with the three dames who were in charge when he took over. First, he had to explain several times exactly where he perched in the family tree. Was it suitable, the ladies then rhetorically enquired, that Cheval-Blanc should be managed by a Lurton? Did he have any other names? What, for instance, was his mother's maiden name? One can but imagine the consternation when Lurton replied that his mother's maiden name was, in fact, Lafitte.

The Cheval-Blanc estate now occupies some forty-one hectares, of which thirty-five are under vines. These are planted in the ratio sixty per cent Cabernet Franc (known as Bouchet in St-Emilion), thirty-nine per cent Merlot, and one per cent Cabernet Sauvignon.

The wine is now made in concrete vats, dating from 1964, and housed in a clean new cellar above which is a terrace from which one can view the vineyard, and behind which is a reception area. The whole effect is cool and refined, a discreet atmosphere of quality.

Cheval-Blanc, the only great wine in the world to be made primarily from Cabernet Franc, is always a wine of great appeal. Its lack of Pauillac backbone and tannin makes it a wine easy to appreciate when young. Yet the richness and abundance of fruit are balanced with plenty of body, and the regular use of new oak adds to the substance while mixing with the spicy, fruit-oaky taste of the Merlot grape to create cigar-box and other complex but elusive flavours.

All in all, Cheval-Blanc is a first-class, and very consistent wine which has hardly ever not produced wines of *grand cru* quality. And it keeps remarkably well. From the 1988 vintage, a second wine, Le Petit Cheval, has been introduced. Previously what was rejected from the *grand vin* was labelled merely as St-Emilion.

Haut-Brion

BORDEAUX

PREDATING THE FAMOUS QUOTE ABOUT HAUT-BRION FROM SAMUEL PEPYS CITED BELOW, HISTORIANS HAVE RECENTLY UNCOVERED A REFERENCE TO THE WINE IN KING CHARLES II'S CELLAR IN 1661.

Haut-Brion can claim to be the senior wine-producing estate in the whole of the Bordeaux area. Not only was it the first to establish itself, and not only did it fetch a much higher price than the other First Growths for nearly a century after, but it was the first single-property Bordeaux wine to be mentioned in English literature or any other records.

This is Samuel Pepys' diary entry on April 10, 1663: "...to the Royal Oake Taverne... And here drank a sort of French wine called Ho Bryan, that hath a good and most particular taste that I never met with." At the time the estate was owned by a wealthy Bordeaux parliamentarian called Arnaud de Pontac.

Between the Pontacs in the 1660s and the Dillons, who acquired the property in 1933 and are still the owners today, Haut-Brion passed through a number of hands. It was briefly owned by Talleyrand, foreign minister of France, in the first decade of the nineteenth century. Various other aristocrats and financiers were involved. But in the early 1930s, following phylloxera, World War I, and the Depression, there were three atrocious vintages. Profitability was at an all-time low. Haut-Brion was put up for sale. The purchaser was an American financier, Clarence Dillon, who paid 2.35 million francs, a little over £100,000 at the rate of exchange ruling at the time. In 1962, the company Domaine Clarence Dillon SA was transferred to Douglas Dillon, former U S Ambassador and finance minister under Kennedy, and the president is now his daughter Joan, Duchesse de Mouchy, aided by her son Robert, Prince of Luxembourg. In 1983 the Dillons bought the neighbouring La Mission Haut-Brion property, the estate of which is run in parallel with that of Château Haut-Brion.

Haut-Brion lies in what was once the suburbs of Bordeaux and, in the famous 1855 Classification of Bordeaux, was the only *premier cru* property to be located outside the Médoc. The last sixty years have seen an extensive programme of modernization of Château Haut-Brion under the direction of the resident *administrateurs*, the Delmas family. Georges Delmas arrived at Haut-Brion in 1921, his son Jean-Bernard took over in 1960, retired in 2002, and is the current director of affairs, and his son Jean-Philippe is currently at the helm.

In 1961, Haut-Brion did something revolutionary. The wooden fermentation vats were

OPPOSITE *Haut-Brion's château was built in 1550 and enlarged some 200 years later*

replaced with stainless steel, Haut-Brion being the pioneer in this respect among the top estates of the Bordeaux region. In the mid-1990s, following what one might call a trial run at La Mission Haut-Brion, Jean-Bernard replaced the 1961 vats with new ones. They are still squat and cubic in shape, but one lies directly above a somewhat smaller second one. The wine is fermented in the top vat. When the time comes to run off the free juice from the *marc* of pips and skins, one just has to open a tap. Hey presto! With no pumping necessary, the juice in the top vat is run off into the one below. "Winemaking is a hands-off process," says Jean-Bernard. "The less manipulation the better."

I asked Jean-Bernard to outline his winemaking methods. Green harvesting? "We did this for the first time at Haut-Brion in 1987. The choice of the date, if this technique is to be successful, is very important. Too soon and the remaining fruit will swell to fill the gap. Too late and you don't get any correspondingly more ripe fruit.

"The best results are obtained if you green harvest half the crop just before the *véraison*, leaving six bunches per vine. This will give you 45–50 hectolitres per hectare (hl/ha)."

And fermentation temperature? "Essentially the winemaker has a choice," Jean-Bernard says. "Lower temperatures favour the freshness and fruit in the wine; higher temperatures will give you a fatter wine, at the expense of the aromas. We find that 30°C (86°F) gives us the perfect balance between the two.

"There are a number of techniques fashionable at the moment: leaving the fruit to get overripe, cold-soaking, using enzymes to extract the colour and the polyphenols, fermenting at high temperatures for an exaggeratedly long time, malolactic in barrel, racking from new wood to new wood after malo, and so on. The results tend to be better with a Merlot-based wine than with a Cabernet one. Is this really Bordeaux? Personally I don't think so. Bordeaux is about harmony, soft tannins, silk rather than bulk, subtlety, elegance, and the ability to age. These new-wave wines lack terroir definition, they could come from anywhere. And they dry out as they age."

The word to sum up the wine of Château Haut-Brion is elegance. One could also add charming and consistent. If Haut-Brion doesn't have the *réclame* (fame) of Lafite or Pétrus, or fetch the same sort of astronomical prices at auction, that is the fault of the consumer. This ignorance is our good luck. On several occasions in recent vintage tastings Haut-Brion has come out top. Moreover it is normally ready for drinking somewhat sooner than the bigger wines of Pauillac and St-Julien. It is a wine I have regularly bought myself, and I confess it to be one of my favourites.

Lafite–Rothschild

BORDEAUX

JUDGED "FIRST OF THE FIRSTS" AT THE TIME OF THE INITIAL 1855
CLASSIFICATION, LAFITE HAS ALWAYS BEEN SEEN AS THE LIGHTEST
OF THE THREE PAUILLAC FIRST GROWTHS, YET WITH GREAT COMPLEXITY.

Some 150 years ago, when the Bordeaux brokers assembled to draw up what was to become the famous 1855 Classification, they agreed that one wine should occupy prime position. Not merely did they assemble five categories of red wines, from First to Fifth, but within each section the wines were listed in order of preference. The first of the Firsts was Château Lafite. Owned at the time by the Ségur family, Lafite was bought in 1868 by the French branch of the Rothschild family associated with the bank in Paris, in whose hands it has remained since.

Wine has probably been produced somewhere on the Lafite estate since before records began. But until the last quarter of the seventeenth century the vine would have been only one of any number of crops. The local *seigneur* would lease out parcels to his tenants, and in those days of mixed farming the peasants would try to be as self-sufficient as possible, planting cereals, vegetables, and other fruits, and rearing chickens, pigs, and cattle. It was not until earlier in the seventeenth century that the Médoc, low lying and subject to equinoxal flooding, was properly drained. This exposed the magnificent gravel mounds we know today. Up to then the most favoured wines of the Bordeaux area came from the *palus*, the alluvial soils close to the rivers Garonne and Dordogne, and the estuary of the Gironde.

But now, with the roots of the vines planted farther inland able to penetrate deep down without getting their feet wet, a new style of Bordeaux began to evolve. It had depth and refinement. It was capable of ageing in bottle to its advantage. It had an individual personality which expressed its origins. The concept of terroir was born, and with it came naturally the desire to isolate these wines, and bottle them separately with a specific site or domaine name. Remarkably quickly this part of the Bordeaux area became monocultural, and the concept of individual château wines, small in number, but high in price, began to find itself a market, especially in the UK.

We can probably date the start of this innovation at Lafite as precisely as October 7, 1670. On this date Jacques de Ségur, owner of Château Calon-Ségur and other estates, married Jeanne de Gasq, a childless widow and proprietor of Lafite. Ségur had a good friend in Arnaud de Pontac, already selling Château Haut-Brion. Manifests of the Lafite estate which date from

ABOVE *Capable of holding
2,200 hogsheads of wine,
Lafite's spectacular second-year
barrel cellar was built in 1989*

ABOVE *Lafite's glorious château dates from the mid-sixteenth century*

later in the 1670s refer to new plantations of vines. I am sure that by 1680 — though we have, as yet, no specific evidence — Lafite was for sale under its own name.

The Lafite vineyard is the most northerly in Pauillac, and includes 4.5 hectares of very old Cabernet Sauvignon across the border in St-Estèphe. The 103 hectares under vine today are planted in the ratio seventy-one per cent Cabernet Sauvignon, three per cent Cabernet Franc, twenty-five per cent Merlot, and one per cent Petit Verdot. The Petit Verdot is rarely used in the *grand vin*, and neither is the Cabernet Franc. Indeed, some vintages (1961, 1994) are 100 per cent Cabernet Sauvignon. In others, such as 1989, there may be as much as one-third Merlot. Although there is no hard and fast rule, normally the *grand vin* contains less than the twenty-five per cent Merlot planted on the estate. Neither is there a fixed view on the proportion of the crop to be declassified to Carruades de Lafite, the second wine. In recent years around forty-five per cent of the total crop becomes Lafite while at the other end of the spectrum fifteen per cent is downgraded to Pauillac.

The average age of the vines is thirty-seven years old, with plots dating from as far back as 1886. One per cent is replanted each season. At harvest, up to 450 pickers descend on the property, so each variety can be collected in optimum condition, a procedure that can take as long as four weeks. The fruit is entirely destemmed before fermentation takes place both in stainless-steel and wooden vats, the latter being preferred for the best parcels. The maturing wine is lodged in a splendid circular underground cellar, constructed in 1988. The wine is bottled after eighteen to twenty months in cask.

Historically Lafite was seen as a lighter wine than the other two Pauillac First Growths, Châteaux Latour and Mouton. The objective, it seemed, was style, finesse, and succulence rather than weight and power. Writing in 1815, Abraham Lawton, a leading broker, described it as "the most elegant and delicate of flavour" of the First Growths. The late Edmund Penning-Rowsell, no mean judge of fine bordeaux, wrote: "the acme of fine claret, well-balanced, elegant, and supple with a fine aroma". My impression is that the wines since 1978 have had a little more *puissance* (not quite the same as power, but certainly suggesting more backbone) than they possessed hitherto. What has not lessened is the sheer aristocratic class that you expect, and indeed usually get, from a prime terroir such as this. This, coupled with a splendid depth of fruit and a marvellous complexity of flavour, is what you will find in a mature Lafite today.

Latour

BORDEAUX

MANY CONSIDER LATOUR TO BE THE MOST BACKWARD OF ALL THE
WINES OF BORDEAUX. YET WHEN IT REACHES MATURITY ALL ARE
AGREED THAT IT IS OFTEN THE MOST PROFOUND.

Latour, unlike many present châteaux, has its origins in a real castle, or at least a fortification, built as one of a chain along the shores of the Gironde to protect the Médoc from the incursions of pirates. This castle was originally square in shape with an enclosed courtyard and a keep of two storeys, and stood roughly on the site of the present-day *chais*. It was burnt down in the 1450s, but from the remains, it is said, today's dovecote, dating from around 1625, was constructed.

The start of Latour's history as a serious wine-producing estate dates from around 1670. In that year it was bought by a Monsieur de Chavannes, a private secretary to Louis XIV, from whom it passed by marriage in 1677 to a Monsieur de Clauzel. It must have been either Chavannes or Clauzel who saw the opportunity of fine wine production. Remarkably quickly, along with a small number of other newly planted estates, this foresight was rewarded. The wine sold under its own name at high prices. It was already a "First Growth". A letter dated October 1723 from a Bordeaux merchant, J. Bruneval, to Henry Powell, wine buyer for the future George II, refers to "four topping growths… La Tour, Lafite, Château Margaux and Pontac (Haut-Brion)".

By this time Latour had passed into the hands of the Ségur family, one of the grandest of the Guyenne. Alexandre de Ségur married Marie-Thérèse de Clauzel in 1696 and, as she was heiress to Latour, the estate joined the many in the Médoc that Ségur owned. In 1760, successors to Ségur divided his estates, and Latour eventually passed into the hands of the Beaumont and Courtrivon families, whose ancestors had married Ségur's daughters.

During the nineteenth century château bottling was at first cautiously, but increasingly widely, adopted; the First Growths led the way, and at Latour this was done from 1863 onwards — the whole crop from 1925. Between these dates the *encépagement* began to adopt its current proportions (seventy-six per cent Cabernet Sauvignon, twenty-two per cent Merlot, one per cent Cabernet Franc, one per cent Petit Verdot), with the elimination of Malbec, Syrah, and lesser grapes, the adoption of Merlot (never found at the beginning of the century), and the focus on Cabernet Sauvignon. The production rose. Finally, a proper if modest château

RIGHT *Latour's tower is well known to anyone familiar with the château label. It is, in fact, a pigeonnier built with the remains of the earlier castle*

was built, a square, compact, two-storey Second Empire building with servants' bedrooms in the mansard roofs.

Official recognition as a *premier cru* came in 1855. Latour was one of four, the same four as enumerated by Bruneval 130 years earlier. And this accolade was followed by a succession of glorious vintages.

The "golden age" of vintages of the mid-nineteenth century was rudely interrupted by the advent of the phylloxera epidemic, followed by an outbreak of mildew. Latour was first hit in 1880, but not until the winter of 1901–2 were any grafted vines planted. By World War I, about half the vineyard was under new vines, although it was probably not until the late 1920s that Château Latour was made from totally grafted wines.

In 1962, the Beaumont and Courtrivon families decided to sell a majority share in the estate. Thus it was acquired by S. Pearson and Sons Ltd, the family company of Lord Cowdray (53.5 per cent), with Harveys of Bristol taking 25.2 per cent and the remainder remaining in France, with the Counts Hubert and Phillip de Beaumont representing the original owners on the board. The famous wine critic Harry Waugh, at that time buyer for Harveys, became another director.

As might be expected — and as happened fifteen years later with Château Margaux — French chauvinism did not allow this sale to foreigners to pass without comment. But, as General de Gaulle is supposed to have remarked (according to that other great claret aficionado, Edmund Penning-Rowsell), Pearson could hardly remove the soil.

Radical change then took place in the vat-house. In 1964, nineteen stainless-steel vats were installed, fourteen of 200-hectolitre capacity and five of 150 hectolitres. Automatic cooling was also introduced, by pouring cold water down the outside of the vat in order to prevent the fermenting temperature rising above 30°C (86°F). At that time *égrappage à la main* — manual removal of the grape-stalks — was also discontinued and a *fouloir-égrappoir*, a crusher-destemmer, was put in. Two years later a second wine, Les Forts de Latour, was introduced.

In March 1989 Allied Lyons PLC, owners of Harveys of Bristol, bought the Pearson's shareholding. Four years later, in June 1993, it was Artemis SA, owned by French industrialist François Pinault, who purchased the controlling stake at a price of £86 million. The director on the spot today is Frédéric Engerer.

How does one describe the wine of Château Latour, a wine which is one of the greatest red wines of the world, which is my — and I imagine others' — yardstick for fine claret? Full, yet never overpowering, let alone coarse, and robust; aristocratic and elegant, without being effete; deep, rich, and powerfully complex in flavour.

Three Léovilles
and a château called Ducru

BORDEAUX

ST-JULIEN MAY NOT BE ABLE TO BOAST ANY FIRST GROWTHS, BUT IT HAS MORE TOP SECONDS THAN ANY OTHER COMMUNE, WITH AN AREA OF THE HIGHEST QUALITY JUST ACROSS THE DITCH FROM CHATEAU LATOUR.

RÉCOLTE 2001

Grand Vin de Léoville
du Marquis de Las Cases
SAINT-JULIEN

APPELLATION SAINT-JULIEN CONTRÔLÉE

PROP⁰ SOCIÉTÉ CIVILE DU CHATEAU LÉOVILLE LAS CASES A SAINT-JULIEN · FRANCE

75 cl   MIS EN BOUTEILLE AU CHATEAU
13 % vol   PRODUCE OF FRANCE

St-Julien lies immediately to the south of Pauillac, the vines of Château Latour and the two Pichons in the latter commune being separated from those in the former parish merely by a drainage ditch. This end of St-Julien is the territory which was formerly the giant Léoville estate, now divided into three: Barton, Las Cases, and Poyferré. A couple of kilometres to the south of this trio, isolated in the middle of its vines, is Château Ducru-Beaucaillou. Between these four estates we have what is best about St-Julien; wines based on Cabernet Sauvignon which combine structure and elegance, ageworthiness and complexity, harmony and richness.

Inevitably, however hands-off you are as a winemaker, wines express not only their origins, but also the personality of their proprietors. Nowhere is this more true than with these four wines. If we look at the percentage of the grapes employed, there is little difference between them: sixty-five per cent Cabernet Sauvignon at Ducru, Las Cases, and Poyferré, seventy-two at Barton; twenty-five per cent Merlot at Ducru and Poyferré, twenty at Barton, nineteen at Las Cases. Odd percentages of Cabernet Franc and Petit Verdot (though none of the latter at Barton) make up the remainder.

The man behind Léoville Las Cases until his untimely death in 2001 was Michel Delon. A widower, Michel was an aloof and private man, meticulous, and a bit of a workaholic. Though genial and hospitable once you got to know him, his public face was rather austere. His overriding ambition was to see Las Cases accepted as the equivalent of a First Growth,

LEFT *The impressive entrance to the bottle cellar at Château Léoville Las Cases*

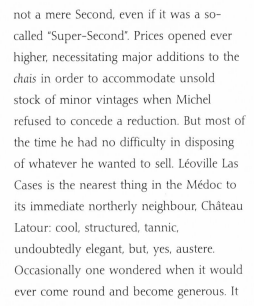

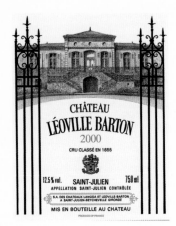

ABOVE *The wine of Léoville Barton made at neighbouring Langoa. This château, an elegant chartreuse, dates from the late 1750s*

not a mere Second, even if it was a so-called "Super-Second". Prices opened ever higher, necessitating major additions to the *chais* in order to accommodate unsold stock of minor vintages when Michel refused to concede a reduction. But most of the time he had no difficulty in disposing of whatever he wanted to sell. Léoville Las Cases is the nearest thing in the Médoc to its immediate northerly neighbour, Château Latour: cool, structured, tannic, undoubtedly elegant, but, yes, austere. Occasionally one wondered when it would ever come round and become generous. It did, but it took time. Michel, now succeeded by his son Jean-Hubert, who intends to relax the austerity just a little, achieved his aim. We have *premier cru* quality here.

Quite a different individual is the elegant, urbane, witty, sometimes deliciously indiscreet Anglo-Irishman Anthony Barton. Now in his seventies, Anthony took over from his late uncle Ronald in 1983. His ancestors in Bordeaux were merchants as well as château owners, as was he, even after the family firm of Barton & Guestier was sold to Seagrams in the 1960s. As a result the Barton pricing policy is generous. "I want my wines to be drunk," he says, "not hoarded as investment museum pieces by millionaires." Léoville Barton is as full-bodied and tannic as Las Cases, but less austere; somehow a little riper and more accessible right from the beginning. It is a very splendid and equally long-living wine. But, and this is where the soil comes in, proving that in general in these parts the nearer to the river the better in the final analysis, Léoville Barton doesn't quite show the same amount of finesse as Las Cases.

The late Jean-Eugène Borie — he sadly died in 2000 — was another individual whose personality was firmly impressed on his wine, his beloved Ducru-Beaucaillou. Jean-Eugène, a shy man with a dry sense of humour, was cautious, indeed conservative, but utterly dedicated to producing the best from his vines. Ducru is not as full as the two Léovilles described above, but its harmony, finesse, and the sheer quality of the fruit flavour are remarkably fine.

Perhaps the odd man out is Léoville Poyferré's Didier Cuvelier. He arrived in 1979 at a time when standards had been allowed to fall and when an unusually high proportion of the vineyard was planted with Merlot. Major investments then ensued, and the *encépagement* was put right. Despite this, though the wines are fine, they do not taste very St-Julien. There is less of a Cabernet Sauvignon flavour; the wine is lusher and more "modern", as if the fruit were picked at a later stage of *sur*-maturity and vinified at a higher temperature. With Poyferré I get less of a correlation between man and wine. It is perhaps no coincidence that at Barton and Ducru, if not at Las Cases, we have the rare example of the proprietor living *in situ*.

RIGHT *The Léoville Poyferré chais lie opposite those of Léoville Las Cases*

RIGHT *The main part of Château Ducru-Beaucaillou, built in the Directoire style, dates from 1820. The towers were added in 1880*

Margaux

BORDEAUX

"I MAY SAFELY ASSURE YOU THAT THERE CANNOT BE A BETTER BOTTLE OF BORDEAUX [THAN MARGAUX] PRODUCED IN FRANCE," SAID THOMAS JEFFERSON IN 1784, A JUDGMENT WHICH HOLDS JUST AS TRUE TODAY.

"The most delicate and the most poetic of the three greatest Médocs", as noted English wine writer Morton Shand wrote in his seminal text *A book of French wine.* "Certainly no wine can equal a fine Margaux in delicate fragrance and subtlety of taste," according to that other connoisseur and doyen of early twentieth-century wine writing, Warner Allen.

The manor or domaine of Margaux dates back to the early Middle Ages. According to one source, there was a fortress here in the thirteenth century, one of a number at intervals up the Gironde estuary protecting the countryside from pirates. Vines were probably planted on a large scale at Margaux in the last half of the seventeenth century, when the proprietors were the D'Aulède family. In some of the earliest references in England to specific vineyard wines, advertisements for the sale in London of prize wine captured from ships during the wars of the Spanish succession, and the records at the beginning of the eighteenth century of purchases made by the Earl of Bristol and prime minister, Sir Robert Walpole, the wine appears frequently and variously as Margaux, Margouze, Margeau, Margau, and even Margot.

After the D'Aulèdes, the ownership of Château Margaux changed frequently. Finally, in 1921, it became a limited company. A syndicate, headed by Pierre Moreau, a Bordeaux broker with Hérault connections, bought out the previous owner, the Duc de la Trémoïlle. From 1925 onwards Fernand Ginestet, a well-known local wine merchant, began to buy the shares of the other members, and his son Pierre finally completed the purchase in 1949.

The Ginestets remained proprietors until 1976. Pierre Ginestet had sold his other interests to concentrate his proprietorial skills on Margaux, but then came the wine madness of 1972 and 1973. The enthusiastic investment of the late 1960s, the opening of important new markets in the USA, plus an excellent vintage in 1970 had generated a bullish air of over-optimism throughout the region. A global energy crisis accompanied by the disastrous vintages of 1972, 1973, and 1974 precipitated a savage slump. Margaux was up for sale. The purchaser was the French supermarket group Félix Potin, whose Greek owner, the late André Mentzelopoulos, was a major shareholder in the French wine firm of Nicolas, and a price of 72 million francs was agreed, to include the three vintages (1974, 1975, and 1976) lying in the château's cellars.

ABOVE *The château of Margaux, renowned as one of the area's most beautiful, dates from 1810 and was built in the First Empire style*

Mentzelopoulos was a financial wizard and a perfectionist, and just the man to rescue Margaux in its hour of need. Land was drained, the stream running through the vineyard was thoroughly dredged, and nearly twelve hectares replanted. A new underground second-year *chai* was constructed. Curiously, however, and contrary to the advice of his good friend, the US author, wine merchant, and fellow château-owner Alexis Lichine (Château Prieuré-Lichine), when the time came to renew the fermentation vats, oak was re-employed instead of introducing stainless steel. Finally Professor Emile Peynaud, lately director of the Bordeaux Institut d'Oenologie, was engaged as an adviser. In 1983 the hugely able Paul Pontallier was appointed wine director.

André Mentzelopoulos, sadly, was unable to see the fruit of his efforts come to full maturity for he died suddenly in 1980 at the age of sixty-six. Undaunted, his widow Laura and daughter Corinne decided to carry on. "At first we continued my father's work out of pride," Nicolas Faith quotes Corinne as saying, "We simply didn't have the right to let it fall."

ABOVE *Venerable bottles from remarkable vintages lie in the château's private cellar*

The visitor approaches Château Margaux through an avenue of trees, leading down to the four Doric pillars and portico incongruously stuck onto the frontage of the mansion as if it had been temporarily borrowed from the front of the British Museum. To the right, beyond the garden, is the main *chai*, an impressive low-ceilinged building about 100 metres (328 feet) long by thirty (ninety-eight feet) wide, and containing the first-year wine maturing away in new oak casks, vividly stained crimson with spillage from the *ouillage*, the weekly topping-up. The barrels here lie on the floor one deep. Adjoining this is the *cuverie* with its twenty-six much larger oak fermentation vats. Adjacent to the first-year cellar is a reception room and small museum, with signed photographs of the famous, menus of state and royal banquets, old vinous knick-knacks, and historical maps and documents. Underneath the courtyard is the second-year cellar.

Of the 150-hectare estate, some eighty-one hectares are planted with vines, in the ratio seventy-five per cent Cabernet Sauvignon, two per cent Cabernet Franc, twenty per cent Merlot, and three per cent Petit Verdot. This is a higher percentage of Cabernet Sauvignon and a lower percentage of Merlot than in pre-Mentzelopoulos times. There is also, rare in the Médoc, a white wine, Pavillon Blanc du Château Margaux.

Two hundred years ago Thomas Jefferson wrote: "I may safely assure you that… there cannot be a better bottle of Bordeaux produced in France." A hundred years later Armand D'Armailhacq, proprietor of the Pauillac Fifth Growth of the same name and perceptive commentator on the wines of his neighbours, wrote of Margaux: "This famous wine is remarkable for its incomparable sweetness of perfume." Today both these observations are as true as ever.

Palmer

BORDEAUX

IF THE WINES OF THE COMMUNE OF MARGAUX ARE CHARACTERIZED
BY THEIR ELEGANCE AND FINESSE, CHATEAU PALMER CAN BE
RIGHTLY CONSIDERED THE MOST ELEGANT OF ALL.

Long before anyone coined the phrase "Super-Second", one château in Cantenac-Margaux —
a *troisième*, not even a *deuxième* — had already achieved Super-Second status. It did so with
a single wine. The château was Palmer. The vintage was 1961.

The 1961s were scarce and very expensive. But fabulous. Almost as soon as the must had
been fermented into wine it became clear that the quality of the Palmer was exceptional —
indisputably First Growth quality.

As time went on, and as the reputation of the wines in bottle began to be accurately
measured by the prices of the then new Christie's wine auctions, Palmer 1961 repeatedly
fetched record levels only matched by the *premiers crus* and their Libournais equivalents. It
continues to do so, currently selling for around £9,000 (US$ 16,784) per case of twelve bottles.

Although the vineyard, as Palmer, dates only from 1814 and the château from 1860, the
origins lie almost a century earlier amidst the ramifications of the family de Gasq. It takes
its name from Major General Charles Palmer, a British Army officer who purchased this
estate at the end of the Napoleonic era.

In 1938, in a dilapidated condition, Château Palmer was bought by a consortium of four
famous local wine names: Sichel, Mahler-Besse, Ginestet, and Miailhe, for, it is said, hardly
more than the cost of a year's upkeep. Since then the latter two families have sold their shares
to the first two. Today the Société Sichel owns thirty-four per cent, while various members
of the Mahler-Besse family hold the remainder.

The vineyards lie in the heart of that part of Haut-Médoc entitled to the appellation
Margaux, both in the commune of Margaux itself and in neighbouring Cantenac. The main
body of the vineyard is directly to the south of that of Château Margaux and on a small
plateau, the first of several that ripple away from the estuary of the river Gironde. Here the
soil is at its most refined, consisting almost entirely of rough gravel with little in the way of
what would serve as nourishment to other crops. The vine has to delve deep but, in doing so,
picks up minute traces of minerals which combine to give the wine its complexity of flavour
and nuances of character.

There are some fifty-two hectares of productive vineyard. As with many Margaux properties, the proportion of Merlot in the *cépage* is relatively high. The mix at present is roughly forty-seven per cent Cabernet Sauvignon, forty-seven per cent Merlot, and six per cent Petit Verdot. The Cabernet Franc — there used to be seven per cent or so in the 1980s — has now been grubbed up. It has not been replaced. The Petit Verdot, like the Cabernet Franc, is not being replanted. As the late Peter Sichel used to say, "In the poor years, when you need it, it doesn't produce ripe and concentrated grapes. In the years when it does, it is superfluous."

There is nothing coarse or robust about a Palmer. Though it may lack body in poor years and, indeed, never have the power of a good Pauillac, there is a finesse, a silkiness, alloyed with a soft fruit and violets perfume of unmistakable and unforgettable delicacy.

It is no exaggeration to state that Palmer, since the war, has consistently produced wine to rank with the very best of the Médoc. Indeed, in 1961 and again in 1966, as I said at the outset, the wine is certainly of First Growth quality. How then to describe it?

As with all the best Margaux, it is never overpowering, never very full in body, yet it is perfectly balanced; aristocratic and accessible while still young, in maturity it attains a soft, generous, almost velvety character, a bouquet of elegant, rich, complex fruit, and a finish of delicate distinction. Would that there were more wines like it!

Pétrus

BORDEAUX

THE MOST SOUGHT-AFTER OF ALL BORDEAUX, PETRUS DRAWS ITS
REMARKABLE CONCENTRATION FROM TWO UNIQUE SELLING POINTS:
ITS PURE MERLOT COMPOSITION AND ITS PECULIAR SOIL.

Château Pétrus is Bordeaux's most expensive and sought-after red wine, but its fame is relatively recent. It was Madame Edmond Loubat, who became sole proprietor by about 1945, who really achieved top-growth status for her beloved Pétrus. The late Edmund Penning-Rowsell, one of the world's greatest Bordeaux experts, described her as "a woman of great personality, who never made the mistake of underestimating the value of her product". Convinced that her wine was second to none in Bordeaux, she was determined that everyone else should recognize it. She asked very high prices for her wine and eventually her clients accepted. In this, she had a good ally in the redoubtable late Jean-Pierre Moueix.

Moueix is the second, complementary part of the Pétrus phenomenon. Starting as merely the proprietor of Château Fonroque in St-Emilion but finding no négociant interested in his wine during the 1930s, he set up as one himself. Today, the business owns farms for an absentee landlord, or has the marketing rights in part or in exclusivity for the majority of the Right Bank's top properties. The estates they own include Trotanoy, Hosanna, La Fleur-Pétrus, and La Grave in Pomerol as well as Magdelaine in St-Emilion. Moueix has been the sole agent for Pétrus since 1947.

Madame Loubat had no children and two heirs, the only children of each of her two sisters, a Madame Lily Lacoste and a Madame Lignac. These two did not get on and before Madame Loubat died in 1961, she gave one share in Pétrus to Jean-Pierre Moueix in order both to enable him to have a say in the management of the property, and to make an exact division of the remainder between the heirs. Moueix bought Madame Lignac's shares in 1964 and was, effectively, the man in charge since then. Jean-Pierre's son Christian is responsible for managing the château, while the viticulture is delegated to Michel Gillet, and the winemaking to *oenologue* Jean-Claude Berrouet.

The Pétrus secret begins with soil. While across the road at La Fleur-Pétrus the soil is partly gravel — as it is in part of the vineyards of Cheval-Blanc and Figeac, and elsewhere in Pomerol there are patches of sand — at Pétrus the soil is clay with a curious blue tinge to it. Underneath this clay is a sub-soil of gravel and underneath this is an impermeable layer of hard iron soil known as *crasse de fer* or *machefer*.

ABOVE *The château is modest,*
merely the chai plus a couple of
reception rooms

ABOVE *The Pétrus vintage
is picked in two successive
afternoons, when the fruit is
at its optimum ripeness*

Planted in this soil are the vines. At Pétrus, the *encépagement* is particular to the property and almost unique in Bordeaux — practically 100 per cent Merlot. While there is five per cent Bouchet (Cabernet Franc) in the vineyard, the wine from these vines is not always used in the *grand vin* blend, for it is only in exceptional years that the Bouchet gets really ripe. Pétrus, then, is a 100 per cent Merlot wine.

The vineyard is not large. Bounded by the other top growths of Pomerol — La Conseillante and L'Evangile to the St-Emilion side, Vieux Château Certan to the southwest, and La Fleur-Pétrus to the west, it measures a mere 11.5 hectares. Until 1969 it was smaller but in that year five hectares were acquired from the best soils of northern neighbour Château Gazin.

Château Pétrus is fermented traditionally in concrete vats which, with a further maceration on skins lasts for eighteen to twenty-five days. This produces a big, sturdy, very rich wine which, despite the amount of Merlot, will not only last but does not take one immediately to the St-Emilion/Pomerol side of Bordeaux. This comes later, when one realizes that the wine, though incredibly, almost overpoweringly powerful and full in body, does not have the austere backbone of the Médoc and does taste distinctively of very concentrated Merlot, not Cabernet.

The first thing that strikes one about Pétrus is its incredible intensity. With concentration comes power. Pétrus is a big wine yet without being massively, austerely tannic in the same way as a young Latour or Mouton-Rothschild: rich and full and sturdy and, as I have said, not immediately redolent of the Libournais despite the quantity of Merlot in the *encépagement*. Pétrus, above all, is a wine of enormous fruit. The fruit dominates the oak, it dominates the tannin. This is as it should be. It can also overpower the taster.

It is perhaps academic to attempt to answer the question of which château produces the greatest bordeaux of them all. Do you measure "the greatest" in terms of prices fetched at auction? If so, what would be the effect if Pétrus were deprived of its rarity value and produced as much as Château Lafite? Even if you were to tot up the marks given for the top Bordeaux in horizontal tastings and found that Pétrus was marginally higher, on average, than the other First Growths, would this really matter? Is it not, perhaps, at this level, a question of personal taste? Speaking for myself, there are moments when I consider Pétrus the greatest red wine produced in Bordeaux and others when I don't. It is an unanswerable question.

Trotanoy

BORDEAUX

WITH ITS PROFOUND, RICH CONCENTRATION AND ARISTOCRATIC FRUIT, TROTANOY, THE JEWEL IN THE CROWN OF THE JEAN-PIERRE MOUEIX FAMILY, IS ARGUABLY THE SECOND-BEST WINE IN POMEROL.

The derivation of the name "Trotanoy" comes from the medieval French *"trop anoi"* or *"trop ennuie"*: literally, too much bother, too wearisome. The soil is a very dense mixture of clay and gravel, which tends to solidify as it dries out after rain to an almost concrete-like hardness; not an easy task to plough, particularly in the pre-tractor days of a single plough-share pulled by a horse or an ox.

Trotanoy lies on the western edge of the central and highest slope of Pomerol. In the middle of this plateau lies Château Pétrus, ringed by most of the rest of the leading properties of the commune: Lafleur, La Fleur-Pétrus, Gazin, L'Evangile, La Conseillante, Petit-Village, and Vieux Château Certan. Continue west for a few hundred metres and you will come across the simple but elegant, white-painted, two-storey farmhouse flanked by its *chais* at the end of an avenue of trees and at the centre of a small nine-hectare vineyard of impressively old vines. This is Trotanoy, owned since 1953 by the family of Jean-Pierre Moueix, and producer of one of the most impressive, deeply concentrated, and profound wines of the entire Bordeaux area.

The Moueix business is one of the success stories of Bordeaux. As the grand Chartron firms have declined in fortune, been taken over and totally changed in character, or even ceased to exist, *Etablissements* Jean-Pierre Moueix has gone from strength to strength.

As well as Pétrus and Trotanoy, J.P. Moueix owns, farms, or exclusively distributes the following splendid array of Pomerol and St-Emilion wines: Latour-à-Pomerol, La Fleur-Pétrus, La Grave-à-Pomerol, Hosanna (formerly Certan-Giraud), Lagrange, Lafleur, and Magdelaine, as well as a host of minor Libournais properties.

Leading the Moueix team from the production point of view are Christian Moueix, Jean-Pierre's son, and oenologist Jean-Claude Berrouet. This is a formidable team, and one able to apply precisely the same perfectionism to the wines of Trotanoy as they do to Pétrus. As at Pétrus, the small vineyard of Trotanoy is picked in a couple of days, when the entire Moueix staff of some 180 people can be deployed to pick the grapes at the optimum point of ripeness. They even delay the harvesting each day until after lunch. By then the dew has evaporated, the berries are dry and warm, and the juice therein a half-degree of potential alcohol riper.

The Trotanoy vineyard slopes gently to the west. The soil at the highest point of exposure contains a good proportion of gravel, becoming progressively more clayey as the elevation declines. Similarly to Petrus, under this clay is a sub-soil of sandy gravel, and this lies on an impermeable layer of hard, iron-rich soil known as *crasse de fer* or *machefer*.

The Berrouet approach to winemaking is classic. Not for him are modern fads such as micro-oxygenation, nor an exaggerated use of new oak. He prefers to pick while there is a good level of acidity in the fruit, rather than at the point almost of overripeness. Moreover, vinification temperatures are on the low side and the length of maceration not excessive. "What I am looking for", he says, "are wines which are relaxed, with energy, freshness, and elegance. Above all we at J.P. Moueix seek an expression of the *terroir*".

Even by "classed growth" standards — there has never been an official classification of Pomerol — the average age of the vines at Trotanoy is impressively old. When Jean-Pierre Moueix bought Trotanoy in 1953, the vineyard consisted entirely of vines which were twenty-five years old; since then little has been replanted. Trotanoy was lucky enough to largely escape the terrible frosts of February 1956.

There are now 7.2 productive hectares in total, since one plot is currently vacant, awaiting replanting. Ninety per cent are Merlot, ten per cent are Bouchet (as Cabernet Franc is known in the Libournais).

Trotanoy is made in much the same way as Pétrus. It is vinified in small concrete vats, with the fermentation taking about a week or ten days, followed by a further week's maceration with the skins. Up until the early 1980s, between ten and thirty per cent of the stalks, according to the vintage, were added to give the wine more muscle and tannin. Since then the fruit has been entirely destemmed. Maturation is in oak, of which one-third is new. Not for the Moueix 200 per cent new oak, as for some so-called "modern wines". The cellars are also used for the manufacture and maturing of Château Lagrange, another Moueix wine.

Old vines produce little, but produce well. Production is rarely more than two *tonneaux* per hectare, rather than as much as four or five in some prolific properties. In the short year of 1977, the total was as low as ten *tonneaux*; in the abundant vintage of 1982, only twenty-seven.

Trotanoy is a profound and richly concentrated wine with plenty of depth and very classy, almost creamy, fruit. Though it has power and weight, and will certainly last, it is never as dense as Pétrus itself, or Lafleur. Nor does it have the Cabernet-Sauvignon-inspired backbone of Vieux Château Certan. In some vintages — 1975, for instance; even 1982 — it comes forward to make very agreeable drinking rather quicker than many of its peers. But so does Magdelaine, the Moueix *premier grand cru* St-Emilion. This is the result of the high proportion of Merlot. But it keeps very well, as the tasting notes will show.

burgundy

The word terroir could have been created for Burgundy. With Chardonnay at its most poised and eloquent, the unpredictable Pinot Noir shows unparalleled finesse, delicacy, and depth of character.

Anne Gros

BURGUNDY

BORN INTO A FAMILY OF WINEMAKERS, ANNE GROS IS ONE OF THE NEXT
GENERATION. IN THE LAST FIFTEEN YEARS SHE HAS ESTABLISHED HER
DOMAINE AMONGST THE TOP HALF-DOZEN IN ALL OF BURGUNDY.

Vosne-Romanée is a commune rich in the finest of vineyard sites — the *grand cru climats* as they are known — and a village replete with growers of the highest quality. One of the longest-established of this first division, owners *inter alia* of the monopoly of an excellent *premier cru*, Clos des Réas, and no less than two hectares — one-quarter — in the best part of the Richebourg vineyard, one of the grandest *grands crus* of them all, is the Gros family. There are now four separate Gros exploitations: Domaine Michel Gros, Domaine Gros Frère et Soeur, Domaine Anne Gros, and Domaine A.F. Gros.

The grandfather of Anne Gros was Louis Gros, who died in 1951. For a while the domaine continued to be run in common by his four children: Gustave, Jean, François, and Colette. François did the paperwork and managed the finances, Jean looked after the vines, and Gustave ran the cellar. Sadly none of the three men seems to have enjoyed the best of health. Nevertheless, with the exception of Gustave, who died in 1984, this generation still survives, though it has been the next generation that has been making the wine for some time.

In 1963, when François got married, the Louis Gros domaine was split up. Jean received the Clos des Réas and part of the Clos de Vougeot Maupertuis, the rest of the Maupertuis went to François, and Gustave and Colette, neither of whom had married, pooled their interests together under the name Gros Frère et Soeur, and took over the Grands-Echézeaux and the larger Musigni section of the Clos de Vougeot. The Richebourg holding was divided.

In the early 1990s Jean Gros officially retired (though the wine had for some time been made by his eldest son Michel) and his estate was divided amongst his children. Michel retained the Clos des Réas and the Clos de Vougeot, while his daughter Anne-Françoise took on the Richebourg. This is made by her husband, François Parent of Pommard, and is sold under the label A.F. Gros. Meanwhile the second son of Jean and Jeanine Gros, Bernard, had been responsible for the Gros Frère et Soeur exploitation since the early 1980s. In 1988 François's daughter Anne took over from her father.

Anne Gros, Michel's cousin, almost comes from a different generation. She was born in 1966, and graduated from wine school only in 1985. Prior to this, most of her father François's

ABOVE *Anne Gros's Clos de Vougeot vines lie in the best section of this fifty-plus-hectare vineyard: Maupertuis. To the right of this wall, upslope, lies Grands-Echézeaux*

wine was sold off in bulk. Anne's wines have been entirely domaine-bottled only since 1990. Anne Gros's wines are either generic and village, or *grand cru* (0.98 hectares Clos de Vougeot; 0.6 hectares Richebourg). She has no *premier cru* wine. There, in the new *cuverie* she had built behind her parents' house in the same *rue des communes* in Vosne-Romanée that houses the Michel Gros winery, we have a little less destemming than *chez* Michel, natural yeasts, up to 100 per cent new wood for the *grands crus,* and fifty per cent for the village Vosne-Romanée and Chambolle-Musigny. The domaine, however, is a lot smaller than Michel's, at six hectares.

The wines, though, are brilliant. She has learned fast. Today her Richebourg is one of the truly great wines of Burgundy. It is a wine of great purity, splendid intensity, and delicious fruit. Like her cousin's wines, these are Pinot Noirs of finesse rather than power. At their best they are very fine indeed.

Armand Rousseau

BURGUNDY

THE ROUSSEAU ESTATE IS NOT ONLY RICH IN *GRANDS CRUS* BUT,
UNLIKE MOST OF BURGUNDY, THE PARCELS ARE ALL SIZEABLE.
THIS MAKES IT EASIER TO BE AS PERFECTIONIST AS POSSIBLE.

When it comes to the wines of Chambertin and Chambertin Clos de Bèze, Burgundy is a minefield. As can be the way with this highly divided region, large portions of both vineyards are owned by underachievers. There is, of course, one major exception. This is Armand Rousseau. Rousseau is one of the very small number of Burgundy estates to which I would unhesitatingly award three stars. Indeed, as far as Chambertin and Clos de Bèze are concerned, you could even argue that there is Rousseau, and then there are the rest.

There are few finer domaines in the Côte d'Or than that of Armand Rousseau. With land in Le Chambertin itself, the *grands crus* Chambertin Clos de Bèze, Mazis, and Chapelle, and the *premiers crus* Clos St-Jacques and Les Cazetiers, all in Gevrey, as well as in the *grand cru* Clos de la Roche in Morey-St-Denis, this fourteen-hectare estate can boast some of the finest sites in the northern part of the Côte. The vines are old, the yield low, and the winemaking perfectionist — and the wines themselves are stunning.

Charles Rousseau himself — he was born in 1923 and took over on his father's death in a car accident in 1959 — is one of nature's gentlemen. Small, ebullient, and shrewd, he is generous with his time and his willingness to impart information. He has the refreshing ability to be dispassionate about the quality of both his own and his neighbours' wines.

Charles may now be eighty-two but he shows absolutely no signs of retiring. Two of his children are now taking some of the weight off his shoulders: his son Eric, in the vineyards and now, increasingly, in the cellars, and his daughter Corinne, on the sales and marketing side.

It all starts in the vineyard. The average age of the vines is deliberately kept high: sixty years in Le Chambertin; forty-five in Clos de Bèze. Every year Charles Rousseau rips out about a sixth of a hectare across his domaine — a few vines here, a few vines there — to maintain this important average. The object, of course, is to keep the harvest low and the concentration of the vines high. In his Clos St-Jacques, for instance, his average yield, the *rendement*, during the 1990s was under 30 hl/ha. Even in the prolific 1996 vintage it was only thirty-five.

Vinification takes place in open stainless-steel vats. Rousseau uses about fifteen per cent of the stems, not so much for the extra tannins the stems will add to the must, but for physical

ABOVE *The Clos St-Jacques vineyard*
with its elegant cabotte, where
vineyard workers can shelter. The
limestone cliffs in the distance are the
base rock of the Burgundy region

ABOVE For wines of this quality, eliminating the sub-standard fruit by careful sorting is essential

reasons, to give aeration to the mixture of juice, skins, and pulp. To vinify all the stems would be a grave mistake, in Rousseau's view. You would get too much tannin, and tannins of the wrong, hard, and unripe sort, as well as an excess of bitter acidity.

Maceration takes place for about a fortnight, the temperature being controlled at a maximum of 31°C (88°F), with *pigeage* and *remontage* (treading down and breaking up of the pulp, and pumping over the juice) twice a day. The wine is then decanted into a fresh vat or straight into cask to await the malolactic fermentation. There is 100 per cent new oak from the woods of Allier for the Chambertin, the Clos de Bèze, and the Clos St-Jacques (which, like others who have holdings here, Rousseau considers better than his other *grands crus*), and sixty per cent for the rest of the top wines. Charles likes to have the malos completed by early spring, so he can then rack the wine (leaving any lees or sediment behind by drawing off the clear wine) and move it to a lower, deeper cellar, so he keeps the cellar temperature at 15°C (59°F) during the winter. There is a second racking in September. Bottling normally takes place between eighteen months and two years after the harvest; the lesser wines in May, the top wines in September.

What exhilarates me about Rousseau's wines is their concentration and their class. The intensity, naturally, is readily apparent in rich, structured vintages such as 1990, 1993, 1995, 1996, and 1999. The class is not only obvious in these vintages, but in lighter years such as 1992 and 1994. Not being dominated by excessive amounts of unripe tannins, as perhaps you might find in a claret in a less ripe vintage, now that they have softened up, wines from these years are surprisingly good. (Only in 1997, and to a lesser extent in 1998 do I feel Rousseau's wines miss out a bit.) These are the proof of a thesis I have put forward elsewhere: go for old vines and expert winemaking in the poorer vintages. You will get much more interesting wine than by buying lesser, village examples in a so-called great vintage.

Comte Georges de Vogüé

BURGUNDY

WITH ITS DELICACY AND FRAGRANCE, MANY FEEL THAT MUSIGNY IS
HOME TO BURGUNDY'S GREATEST RED WINE. WITH A LIGHT TOUCH,
COMTE GEORGES DE VOGUE PRODUCES THE FINEST OF THESE.

Delicate, feminine, and fragrant, the epitome of finesse; lace, silk, and taffeta; violets and dog-roses; raspberries and blackcurrants with a finish of liquorice; amplitude and generosity; intensity without a trace of hardness. All this has been said by those attempting to describe the taste of Musigny. It goes further: an ode by Keats; an oboe solo from the Sixth Symphony of Beethoven; a Fabergé egg. What is it about Musigny that excites the imagination to such realms of fantasy?

Musigny is indeed an individual and distinctive wine. It is totally dissimilar from the other *grand cru* of Chambolle, Bonnes Mares. But then the two are separated by a village, the valley of the tumbling river Grosne, and several hundred metres of vineyard. But it is also quite different from its contiguous neighbour, the Clos de Vougeot. Musigny lies higher up the slope, at a point where the rise becomes distinctly steep. The soil is stony and thin, with barely thirty centimetres (11.8 inches) of surface earth before you strike the crumbling limestone rock underneath. There is red clay in the upper part of the *climat*, rare in itself, but in general there is less clay than farther down or in Bonnes Mares, less nitrogenous matter, and hence more breed, and more definition in the wine, but less structure. Friable is the soil of Musigny, and this contributes to the fragrance of the wine.

And the wine, when it is good, is perfumed and silky-smooth, not rugged and masculine. The tannins are there, but they are supple; the vigour is present, but the feel is essentially soft. If Musigny has a similarity with any other *grand cru*, it is with Romanée-St-Vivant, just as the wines of Chambolle find their echo in those of Volnay in the Côte de Beaune.

Le Musigny consists of two sub-*climats*, Le Musigny itself and at the same altitude next door to the south, Les Petits-Musigny. In addition a couple of isolated parcels of the Combe d'Orveau seem to have been able to prove to the authorities that they had always produced Musigny wine and have been added on. Altogether this comprises 10.86 hectares. The lion's share, 7.25 hectares, almost seventy per cent, including the totality of Les Petits-Musigny, belongs to the Domaine Comte Georges de Vogüé. Not for nothing does this estate proclaim itself the Domaine des Musigny.

OPPOSITE *Harvesting in Le Musigny with the château of Clos de Vougeot in the background*

Following the death of the late Comte Georges de Vogüé in 1987, the estate is owned by his grandchildren. It is managed by Jean-Luc Pépin and the wine made by François Millet.

Located in one of the thin side roads in the heart of the village, you gain access to the large Vogüé courtyard through a fifteenth-century porch. Opposite you lie the *chais*. Beneath the *chais* is the cellar, a vast, vaulted room, replete with barrels of young wine, and cool and tranquil as all cellars should be.

The domaine itself comprises 12.4 hectares. As well as the 7.25 hectares of Musigny, there are 2.75 hectares of Bonnes Mares, located entirely in the southern, Chambolle end of this *climat*, 0.6 hectares of Amoureuses, 1.8 hectares of *premier cru* land (Baudes and Fuées), and a small parcel of village wine. The Musigny vines average forty years — it is all sold as Musigny Vieilles Vignes; the rest twenty-five to thirty years old.

How do they make the wine? As François Millet will hasten to assure you, flexibility is the key. The first thing is a low *rendement*: 30 hl/ha is the paramount objective. After that the fruit is largely if not totally destemmed. It depends on the vintage, the origin of the grapes, and the ripeness of the stems themselves. Fermentation takes place at relatively high temperatures — above 30°C (86°F) rather than below, and where possible the length of the maceration is prolonged. There is a judicious, but not excessive, use of new wood, only a light filtration, and the wines are bottled after a year to eighteen months.

And the wine? In my opinion, Le Musigny produces the greatest red wine in Burgundy. The de Vogüé example is simply the best of all of them.

Comtes Lafon

BURGUNDY

CHARDONNAY IS ARGUABLY THE GREATEST WHITE WINE GRAPE VARIETY IN
THE WORLD. USING ECO-FRIENDLY PRACTICES AND CALLING UPON FRUIT
FROM BURGUNDY'S FINEST SITES, LAFON'S ARE SOME OF THE VERY BEST.

The Domaine des Comtes Lafon is not only indubitably three-star, but in my view the world's greatest white wine domaine. At the helm, in the person of the forty-seven-year-old Dominique Lafon, it has one of the most talented winemakers in all Burgundy and one of its most enquiring minds. It is only recently, though, that the Lafon domaine has been fully in charge of its vines and its wines. For most of the postwar period the land was leased out on a *métayage* (share-cropping) basis to other local *vignerons* who kept up to half the crop produced.

In 1865 Jules Lafon, a lawyer by profession, arrived in Burgundy from his native Gers — he was born in Auch, in the middle of Armagnac country — to take up the position of *inspecteur des finances* in Dijon. He wooed and married a Marie Boch from Meursault, and in 1867 the couple set about constructing a substantial Victorian home in a little park in the northern outskirts of Meursault.

Jules Lafon was rich and successful. He was also an intransigent Roman Catholic. When church and state were separated in 1905, he was unwilling to allow his tax inspectorial post to be used to force the ecclesiastics to declare their wealth. Instead he resigned his position and retired into private legal practice. In gratitude the Vatican appointed him a Pontifical Count.

Perhaps the greatest of Jules Lafon's achievements was the creation of La Paulée de Meursault, the last and infinitely the most enjoyable of the three gastronomic festivities which surround the Hospices de Beaune auction in late November. In 1923, being mayor of Meursault, he had the idea of reviving the traditional end-of-harvest meal when the owner celebrates the vintage with his workers. Lafon invited thirty-five of his friends to a small feast. Today some 600 guests manage to squeeze their way into the Château de Meursault, each bearing an interesting old wine or three. It is the greatest bottle party in the world.

In 1978 Count Jules's grandson, Dominique, enrolled at the Lycée Viticole at Beaune and began to be involved in the winemaking, alongside his father René. Between 1982 and 1986, having completed his oenological and viticultural studies, he worked for renowned wine broker Becky Wasserman in Bouilland, arranging his holidays so that he would be available during the harvest. Gradually he took over responsibility for the wines. René's last vintage was 1982.

LEFT *The Lafon mansion is
one of many fine buildings
in Meursault*

ABOVE *Old vintages lying in the
Comtes Lafon private cellar.
Well-made white burgundy can
last for a surprisingly long time*

ABOVE *A typical vintage scene
in Burgundy*

From 1987 onwards the *métayage* arrangements began to come to an end, and Dominique started to become involved in the vineyards as well as in the cellar. Has he changed anything? "Over the last decade the vineyards have been worked Biodynamically [organic in approach, the timing of vineyard activities follows the phases of the moon and treatments are largely homeopathic]. As far as the winemaking is concerned I have not altered things to any great extent. The white wines have always been bottled late. They were kept two years on their lees in the time of my great-grandfather. We are lucky that the cellar is deep and very cold."

The impressive roll-call of Lafon wines and *climats* begins in Volnay: Champans, Santenots, and Clos-des-Chênes, three of the top five *premiers crus* — Caillerets and Taille-Pieds are the others — in the village. In Meursault there are Lafon vines in all three of the top *premiers crus*.

The Charmes is usually the most accessible, the roundest, and the most typically Meursault. This is a wine of honey and hazelnuts and hot buttered toast; all silk and soft pillows. The Genevrières is fuller, often the least appealing in its youth, less sensual, more intellectual. The Perrières is a synthesis of the two, with an element of Puligny floweriness and steeliness: the most complete, the most refined, the most complex.

In 1991 Dominique Lafon finally took back his family's one-third of a hectare of Le Montrachet. Lafon's vines are the most southerly in this famous *climat*, in the Chassagne section. The vines are twenty and fifty years old; the soil a light yellow-brown, almost beige, and very stony indeed. In a good year he will make five *pièces*: 125 cases of the best white wine in the world. All in all the thirteen-hectare Lafon domaine makes just 50,000 bottles a year.

Joseph Drouhin

BURGUNDY

THROUGH A POLICY OF HARD WORK, ASTUTE LAND ACQUISITION, AND DEVOTION TO TERROIR, THE WINES OF DROUHIN ARE SOME OF THE MOST INTENSE, FRAGRANT, AND ELEGANT EXAMPLES TO BE FOUND.

Like most of the top merchants in Burgundy, the firm of Joseph Drouhin subsists for its top wines largely on the produce of its own estate. This measures some seventy hectares, twenty-five or so in the Côte d'Or and forty-five in Chablis. Though the firm dates from 1880, the domaine's origins begin some forty years later. Maurice Drouhin, son of Joseph, came back from the war in 1919 and took over the direction of the business. He decided to specialize at the finer end of the market and to invest in land.

At the time, vineyards were cheap, a lot of them *en friche* (uncultivated), having been allowed to go fallow following the disaster of the phylloxera epidemic. He first acquired the 13.7-hectare Clos des Mouches, a *premier cru* Beaune vineyard at the southern end of the commune, and other local parcels, none of them very far away. In those days horses were used in the vineyards, and as a result there were limits to how far one could travel.

In 1938 Maurice Drouhin bought almost two-thirds of a hectare of Clos de Vougeot. It was his first venture outside the purlieus of Beaune. It was not, at that stage, a profitable move.

Robert Drouhin, nephew and heir-apparent, was born in 1933. It was intended that he should serve a long apprenticeship before succeeding his uncle at the family firm, and to this end after military service Robert enrolled himself at wine school to take an oenological degree. It was not to be. In 1957 Maurice Drouhin suffered a stroke. Robert was thrown into the deep end at the tender age of twenty-four.

He continued his uncle's policy of vineyard acquisition. In 1961, the year he got married, he bought vines in Chambolle, including some Amoureuses, Bonnes Mares, and Musigny. Parcels of Volnay and Corton followed, as did Clos de Bèze, Echézeaux, Grands-Echézeaux, and Bâtard-Montrachet. Moreover, since 1947 Drouhin has farmed and marketed the estate of the Marquis de Laguiche, owner of the largest portion of the Montrachet *grand cru*. In 1968, when the fortunes of Chablis were at their lowest ebb, he started building up what is now an extensive holding in the best part of that commune.

Robert's four children, Frédéric, Philippe, Véronique, and Laurent, are all involved in the business, and at least one has begun to build up vineyards of her own. Véronique, as well

ABOVE *These splendid, vaulted
medieval cellars in the middle of
Beaune once belonged to the
dukes of Burgundy*

ABOVE *The entrance to Drouhin's prized* premier cru *Clos des Mouches vineyard, the first to be bought by Maurice Drouhin after World War I*

as her involvement as winemaker at the Domaine Drouhin winery in Oregon's Willamette valley, is proprietor of the largest segment in the Vosne-Romanée *premier cru* Les Petits Monts, which lies just above the Richebourg *grand cru*.

The Drouhin grapes are partially destemmed, the unstemmed bunches are poured into the vats whole, and the *cuves* cooled to allow forty-eight hours, pre-fermentation maceration. Artificial yeasts are abhorred. "Technically perfect wines which do not reflect the typicity of their terroir have no appeal for me. We may have less consistency but in the long term we have greater elegance, complexity, and fidelity to the earth with the wines we produce at Drouhin," says Robert.

The percentage of new oak is low. "We are not carpenters. We make our wines with grapes, not wood! Oak, properly used, helps determine the personality of the wines and their balance. Nothing should dominate — not alcohol, not tannin, not over-oaked vanillin. Young, these wines might not make as big a statement, but over time they are better."

Drouhin's wines are light in colour, and may seem, to the uninitiated, at first somewhat light on the palate. Delicate is the word used. And feminine.

But this is deceptive. Underneath there is a lot of intensity. Above all there is a great integrity of terroir. Above all there is breeding and finesse. These are fine wines, pure Pinot Noir, never blockbusters. They might not seem very structured, but they are complex and they will certainly keep.

Just under the point where Clos de Bèze becomes Chambertin, sandwiched between Chapelle and the best part of Charmes, you will find Gevrey's smallest *grand cru*, the 2.73-hectare Griotte-Chambertin. Robert Drouhin is the third-largest owner here, with 0.5 hectares, just enough for seven barrels. He acquired this parcel from the commune of Gevrey in 1981.

Everyone assumes that, because a Griotte is a bitter cherry akin to a Montmorency, better for jam rather than plain eating, this is the derivation of the name. A number of famous palates swear by the cherry flavours in the wine. In fact the origin is more prosaic. Griotte is a corruption of *crai* (chalk) as in vineyards called Criot.

The soil here is Bajocian limestone, much weathered, even rotten, mixed with small stones, rich in fossils. When it rains, the vineyard can get very wet, for there are a number of underground streams and springs. But it drains well.

The wine that Griotte-Chambertin produces is never full-bodied, but it has great definition and finesse; real poise, excellent harmony, and a most delicious expression of fruit. It is just the wine to suit the Drouhin style.

Leflaive

BURGUNDY

EMPLOYING INCREDIBLE ATTENTION TO DETAIL, BOTH IN THE FIELD AND
CELLAR, ANNE-CLAUDE LEFLAIVE PRODUCES THE EPITOME OF FINE
WHITE BURGUNDY: PURE, POISED, AND UNDERSTATED.

In 1991 a curious anomaly was rectified. It seemed hardly credible, given that the eight-plus hectares are divided between fifteen different proprietors, that not a single Le Montrachet vine should belong to a domaine based in Puligny. In that year the Domaine Leflaive acquired two *ouvrées*, an area producing just enough fruit to fill one rather over-sized, specially made cask. It was a fitting addition to one of the greatest white wine domaines in Burgundy.

Joseph Leflaive was born in 1870 and was not originally reared to be a *vigneron*. One can imagine, with a family property then at an uneconomic two hectares, that most if not all the Leflaives must have had to earn their living away from the vine. Nevertheless, he did not neglect his patrimony. In the aftermath of the phylloxera epidemic more and more land was falling into disuse as smallholders, unable to replant in a time of depression and falling prices, simply gave up their vineyards. For those with means, the patience, and the foresight, it was a golden opportunity. Between 1905 and 1925 Joseph Leflaive built up his own holdings by acquiring parcels in the most illustrious *climats*: Le Chevalier, Le Bâtard, Les Bienvenues, Les Pucelles, Les Folatières, Les Combettes, and Le Clavoillon.

It was in 1989 that Anne-Claude Leflaive, who runs the estate today, attended a seminar set up by Claude Bourguignon, the well-known agricultural scientist, and Jean-Claude Rateau of Beaune, one of the first local growers to go Biodynamic. She was intrigued. "We were spending lots of money on viticultural treatments at the time," she says, "not always to great effect. I decided to try the system out. We started with one hectare. The results were decisive. We expanded, and since 1997 the domaine has been totally Biodynamic." Many others, Anne-Claude points out, have since followed suit, including top estates such as Lafon, Lafarge, and Pierre Morey in his own vineyards.

OPPOSITE The grand cru vineyard of Bâtard-Montrachet during harvest

You will find the headquarters of Domaine Leflaive behind a heavy wrought-iron gate off one of the several *places* in Puligny. A short walk across the square towards the church and up an alley will take you to the *cuverie* and first-year "cellar". All these are above ground. The water table under Puligny is too high to enable underground cellar construction.

After a severe triage in the vineyard, the grapes are harvested and speedily pressed in two Bücher pneumatic presses, and the must is then allowed to settle overnight. The *crus* are fermented in oak, the lesser wines in wooden *foudres*. The temperature of the fermentation is maintained at 18°C (64°F). The wine then remains in oak for about ten months. Sometime towards the end of the following summer the wines are transferred back — they used to be filtered at this point, but since 1998 no longer — across the village where they are stored in stainless-steel tanks before a light fining with casein. The cold of the second winter helps settle out and clarify the wine and so only a light filtration is necessary, prior to bottling, which takes place around eighteen months after the vintage.

The wood used is both *foudres*, large oak tuns of varying capacity, and *pièces*, the traditional Burgundy 228-litre barrel. About one-third to one-quarter of these *pièces* — Allier or Vosges in provenance, rather than Limousin, which would impart too strong a taste — are annually renewed.

What have Anne-Claude Leflaive and *régisseur* Pierre Morey altered or added since they took over in the 1980s, I ask Anne-Claude.

"I think the most important thing is our attitude towards the vineyards," she says. "Not only are we now totally *Biodynamique*, we now regard each plot as a separate unit. In the time of my father we tended to pick, say, all the Pucelles in one go. Now we treat and harvest all the parcels — and we have thirty-eight — separately. We prune later," she added, "when the sap has already begun to rise. You get less chance of disease that way.

"Another thing we have changed is our attitude towards *bâtonnage* [the stirring of the lees]. We now do this two or three times a week until Christmas. This is rather more than we used to. And because we are stirring the lees up, we find we no longer need to use added yeasts to finish the fermentation properly."

The Leflaive wines are pure, poised, and understated; wines without a suggestion of alcohol even in the richest of vintages. Underneath a subtle, complex, almost deceptive delicacy hides a wine of enormous depth, quality, and concentration. These are great white burgundies.

Leroy

BURGUNDY

A LIFETIME FASCINATION WITH WINE AND A RECENT CONVERSION TO BIODYNAMICS ARE TWO FACTORS THAT CONTRIBUTE TO THE WINES OF LEROY BEING AMONG THE MOST *RECHERCHES* AND EXPENSIVE IN BURGUNDY.

Richebourg
Grand Cru
Appellation Contrôlée
Mis en bouteille au Domaine
LEROY *Propriétaire à Vosne-Romanée Côte-d'Or, France*
13 % vol.   PRODUCT OF FRANCE   75 cl

More than a century ago, in 1868, François Leroy set himself up as a wine merchant in his native village of Auxey-Duresses, just round the corner from Meursault. The business was expanded by his son Joseph, who took over at about the turn of the century, and further developed by the next generation in the person of Henri, born in 1894, who entered the family affair in 1919. Henri diversified into *eaux de vie* and cognac, establishing a model distillery at Ségonzac. As well as fine wine, he sold lesser bulk wine to Germany, where it was made into Sekt — and brandy followed the same path, particularly to Asbach.

During the 1930s Henri became, firstly a client of Domaine de la Romanée-Conti, then a good friend of Edmond Gaudin de Villaine, the *gérant*, and eventually co-owner and joint manager of this famous estate.

Henri Leroy and his wife Simone (*née* Brun) had two daughters, Pauline in 1929, and Marcelle (universally known as Lalou) in 1932. It was the latter, adored and adoring younger daughter, who was to inherit her father's passion for wine.

Lalou, born in Paris, was brought up in Meursault, in the mansion today occupied by her daughter, Perrine. "From the word go I was fascinated," she says. "I was a cellar rat, watching and helping the *cavistes* rack the wines, taste them, bottle them. My mother kept calling me to come out of the cellar to play with my friends like a normal schoolgirl, but as soon as I could I crept back." Henri Leroy, his attention diverted by Domaine de la Romanée-Conti (DRC), had somewhat neglected his négociant business. Lalou remembers 1937s still in cask long after the war. In 1955 she persuaded her father to let her take over. She was twenty-three. "He gave me *carte blanche*," she says. "I started as I meant to go on. I bought finished wine, and only that which pleased me. I insisted on having no contracts, no moral obligations. If the wine wasn't 'extra', I didn't buy it."

In 1974 the co-managership at the DRC passed down a generation, to Lalou, representing her sister (they both owned twenty-five per cent), and Aubert, son of Henri de Villaine, representing his brothers, sisters, and cousins (there are ten of them). From the start this was a fiery relationship. Lalou is not an easy character: emotional, insecure, arrogant, temperamental,

RIGHT *The elegant entrance to Domaine Leroy's Vosne-Romanée headquarters*

ABOVE *The Leroy barrel cellar in Vosne-Romanée*

and combative, she must have been a trial to the pacific, intellectual Aubert. It was a fire awaiting a match. Early in 1992, following a boardroom dispute, Lalou was relieved of her position as *co-gérante*, and the DRC took over responsibility for selling and marketing its wines throughout the world.

Meanwhile, at the other end of Vosne-Romanée lay the headquarters of the twelve-hectare Charles Noëllat domaine. The landholdings were impressive: nearly a hectare of Romanée-St-Vivant, over 1.5 hectares of very well-placed Clos de Vougeot, 0.78 hectares of Richebourg, and substantial *premier cru* vineyards in Nuits-St-Georges (Les Boudots) and Vosne-Romanée (Les Beaux-Monts and Aux Brûlées). But quality was unremarkable and inconsistent. "Yes, the wines they produced were terrible," says Lalou, "But the quality of the vines was great. All honour to Charles Noëllat. The vines were old, reproduced by *sélection massale* [choosing by eye the most robust plants]. I have never seen anything so fine in all of Burgundy."

In 1988 the estate came on the market. Others were interested, but Leroy made a better offer. Things did not stop here. In 1989 Lalou acquired the Gevrey-based twenty-five-hectare Domaine Philippe Rémy. This added 0.4 hectares of Chambertin, 0.57 of Latricières, and 0.67 of Clos de la Roche, as well as *premiers crus* in Gevrey-Chambertin, Les Combottes, and village land in Gevrey and Chambolle. It neatly complemented the Noëllat estate. One year later Lalou increased her holding in Le Musigny by buying a parcel from the Moine-Hudelot family. Some Corton, both red and white, has followed. Today the domaine measures just shy of 22.5 hectares.

In many ways the seemingly hard-nosed Lalou Bize is the last person you might expect to be seduced by any new fad. That Biodynamism is not a fad is proven by the fact that she has joined an increasing number of wineries who have gone not just *Biologique* but the full way.

In fact, the Leroy winemaking methods are deeply traditional. Ploughing is now largely done using horses, to avoid compacting the soil. Pruning is excessively strict. In 2004 there was no *rognage* (clipping of excess vegetation). There is no destemming, a severe *triage* (sorting), two *pigeages* (pressing down of skins) a day — there are automatic plungers available but the cellar team have now reverted to *pigeage à pied* — and a long *cuvaison* at temperatures up to 33°C (91°F). Each vat at Vosne-Romanée is equipped with an internal temperature-controlling stainless-steel coil. One hundred per cent new wood is used. There is no filtration, and not always a fining either. Curiously, the wines are bottled very early: the 2002 and 2003 ten months after the harvest. The wines are excessively expensive, but they can be brilliant.

Louis Jadot

BURGUNDY

LOUIS JADOT OFFERS WHAT IS CERTAINLY THE MOST COMPREHENSIVE AND ARGUABLY ONE OF THE FINEST RANGES OF BURGUNDY. ALL THE TOP WINES COME FROM ITS OWN EXTENSIVE ESTATE.

The firm of Louis Jadot was founded in 1859. It is now one of the largest and most important of the quality Beaune négociants. Today Jadot has a domaine of some sixty-five hectares in the Côte d'Or. They also make and market the wines of the estate of the Duc de Magenta in Chassagne as well as having a number of other local agreements. In total they own vines in forty-three different *premiers* and *grands crus*, plus a seventy-hectare domaine in the Beaujolais.

On the death of the third Louis Jadot in 1962, André Gagey, at the time assistant to Monsieur Jadot, was asked to run the company as regent for Louis-Alain Jadot. Unhappily Louis-Alain was killed in a car crash at the age of twenty-three in 1968. Gagey was appointed general manager and later managing director. In 1985 the Jadot family sold the firm — but not the vineyard — to the Kopf family, owners of Kobrand, Jadot's US agents. Nevertheless Pierre-Henry Gagey, the late André's son, has had a completely free hand, and the firm continues quite unencumbered by outside influences, now vinifying the vast majority of its wines itself under the direction of the able and engaging Jacques Lardière.

Jacques Lardière, youthful, energetic and curly haired, is the genius behind Maison Jadot. He started in 1970, at the age of twenty-three, working alongside an old boy called Forey who was in charge of the cellars. Before too long he had to deal with the problems of the 1971 vintage, a year when hail damaged much of the *côte*. "I am going to have to vinify with the skins for only a very short time, and so at an unnaturally high temperature if I am going to extract any colour," he told André Gagey. "Let me sleep on it" was the response. The next day Gagey gave him the go-ahead, though at first he was doubtful of the results. But when the wines turned out fine, with no lack of colour and substance, and when they later found out that they were the only négociant in Beaune without a single tainted wine, he apologized to Lardière for his initial suspicion. Lardière has had *carte blanche* ever since.

As far as winemaking is concerned, for Lardière there are only a few simple rules and only one single objective. The objective is the expression of the terroir, whether that of a humble Santenay or a grand Clos de Bèze. The way to achieve this is an illogical (on the face of it) mixture of interfering as little as possible and being prepared to take risks. Some of the things

OPPOSITE *Part of the old Jadot cellars in the heart of Beaune*

ABOVE *The modern vinification centre at Louis Jadot in the heart of Beaune*

ABOVE RIGHT *Louis Jadot's holdings include vineyards in forty-three different grands and premiers crus throughout the Côte d'Or*

he does would be shot to bits by the teachers of any wine school. He would be equally criticized for not doing a lot of what he doesn't do.

For the red wines the point at where the eyebrows rise up is when you hear that Lardière doesn't worry if the temperature rises to 35°C (95°F) or even more, a point where most *vignerons* would expect the fermentation to stick and the wine to become infected by vinegar bacteria. He destems the fruit, allows the must to cold-soak for up to five or six days, and ferments in open wooden vats with two *pigeages* a day, using natural yeasts. He also likes to ferment and macerate for as long as a month. Most others are content with half this.

Lardière's attitude to oak is also a little bizarre. The accepted theory is that fine concentrated vintages are balanced by lots of new oak, light vintages dominated by it. *Chez* Jadot the *grands millésimes* are given fifteen to twenty per cent new oak, the *petits millésimes* fifty per cent. It doesn't seem to upset the wine. There is a single racking only, and bottling without either fining or filtration. Here at least we are on secure ground. And Lardière takes care that you realize that every single barrel, every *cuvée*, is tasted and analyzed continually. Nothing is left to chance.

This is a man of passion and sensuality. Wine for him is part of the magic of life. Wine is made by God, but all too often screwed up by the ignorant human, he once said to me. "Look at all the boring wines," he says. "Many of them are technically impeccable, but they have no soul, no personality in them. They could have been manufactured by robots. I sometimes wonder if the people who make them ever taste them. You must use your taste-buds, your imagination, your intelligence. Not a rule book!"

And look at all the Jadot wines, you could reply. They are not all perfect. But on the scale that they are made the overall quality is remarkable, mind-boggling even. Jadot is lucky to have him. And, as customers, so too are we.

Ramonet

BURGUNDY

RAMONET'S BURGUNDIES ARE FINELY CONSTRUCTED, PROFOUND, AND LONG-LASTING, WITH A STREAK OF UNBRIDLED ORIGINALITY THAT ILLUSTRATES THE SHEER CHARACTER OF THE FOUNDER AND HIS FAMILY.

It is the spring of 1978. A small man, seventy-two years of age and very much a peasant, with an old stained pullover, baggy trousers, and the inevitable *casquette* on his head, arrives at a lawyer's office in Beaune. He is about to buy just over a quarter of a hectare — enough to make about 4.5 barrels — of Le Montrachet, the finest white wine vineyard in the world. The vendors are the Milan and Mathey-Blanchet families: gentle people. Pierre Ramonet is a man of the soil. Apart from the occasional meal at some of his clients — Lameloise, Alan Chapel, Troisgros, Bocuse — he never ventures outside Chassagne-Montrachet. He hates the telephone. He rarely writes a letter. Such paperwork that needs to be done is achieved by Mother Ramonet, *née* Lucie Prudhon, whom you will never see dressed otherwise than in black, as befits old ladies throughout France, in an old school exercise book which she keeps in a drawer in her kitchen.

There is the question of payment. "Ah, yes," says Ramonet. He fishes in one pocket for a thick wad of notes, in another for a second, in the back of his trousers for a third, and so on. The stacks of money pile up on the attorney's desk. He has never seen such an amount of *espèces* in his life. "I think you'll find it all there," says Ramonet, uncomfortable in the formal surroundings of the lawyer's office. And he leaves, anxious to return to the familiarity of his cellar and his vines.

"*Père*" Ramonet was more than a character. He was, to use the old cliché — but it is true in this instance — a legend in his own lifetime. More or less from scratch, by dint of sheer hard work and a genius for wine, he built up one of the finest white wine domaines in Burgundy. Today the name of Ramonet is synonymous with top Chardonnay. The allocations for bottles are fought over, for every collector considers it his or her right to own some. They sell at auction for astronomical sums whenever they appear. On the rare occasions, as in January 1995 at the Montrachet restaurant in New York, when someone puts on a special vertical tasting and dinner, the tickets — and they are not cheap — are oversubscribed ten times.

As many people have observed, Ramonet in white is the equivalent of Henri Jayer or the Domaine de la Romanée-Conti in red.

Pierre Ramonet died in 1994 at the age of eighty-eight. He is much missed. But his echo lives on, and the wines, in the able hands of his grandsons Noël (born 1962) and Jean-Claude (1967) since the 1984 vintage (mais *sous ses ordres*, stoutly avers Noël), continue his reputation. They are very fine. More importantly, they are also very individual. A Ramonet wine is a Ramonet wine before it is a Chassagne, or a Bienvenue, or a Bâtard... or a Montrachet.

The cellar, both upstairs and downstairs, is not the neatest, most orderly cellar you have ever been into. Odd bits of machinery, adaptors for pipes, and boxes of this or that lie all over the place. You feel they have never had a tidy-up or thrown anything out. As you squeeze between a beaten-up truck and a redundant pumping machine to get below to sample the wines, you find that the staircase is used as a cupboard for yet more accumulation of bits and pieces. It is like an ironmonger's nightmare.

But all this seems fitting when you meet Noël Ramonet. The man is in his early forties, stocky, usually unshaven, in a dirty old T-shirt and jeans, with piercing blue eyes, a loud voice, and a pre-emptory way of expressing himself. Finesse, order, method, and reflection are alien. Energy, passion, and forthrightness are in his manner. But when you listen, you realize that this is truly a chip off the old block. He reveres his grandfather. But he has his own full understanding of his *métier*. (He has also got one of the most magnificent — and eclectic — private cellars I have ever seen. All bought; none exchanged.)

"*Moins fin mais plus profond*," he will agree with you, when you sample the Chassagne Morgeots white after the St-Aubin, Charmois. And the Boudriottes is more mineral, less fat and heavy, because this is on the semi-*coteaux*, while the Morgeots is in the plain. The Chaumées, despite being young vines, and the Vergers show more finesse. They are properly on the slope. And the Caillerets and the Ruchottes are best of all. "Where the soils are really well drained, as here," explains Noël, "you will always have much less problem with botrytis." This is the heartland of Chassagne white.

Why is there such a sharp contrast between the Bienvenue — composed, accessible, discreet — and the Bâtard — closed, powerful, masculine? After all the vines are adjacent, and the same age. Noël shrugs. You feel he knows the answer. But he can't articulate it. And is his Bâtard his most consistently successful wine? Better even than the Montrachet, which can be totally brilliant, but over the seventeen years since the Ramonets have produced it, certainly not always? Is this a line of questioning you even dare begin?

I find the Ramonet reds refreshingly direct. They are full, ample, and plump, nicely concentrated but succulent. Chassagne reds will never be great, and can be over-extracted. But the Ramonets get theirs right. The whites, on the other hand, are exceptional. Distinctive, full-bodied, and long-lasting, they are rich and masculine, firm and dense, and can be magnificent.

And they can also be flawed. This is a result of risks being taken. But often the flaws are by no means disagreeable; they lend individuality; they give character; they add an element of danger. For me, a great wine often *does* have something just a little bit "wrong" about it. And a squeaky-clean "perfect" wine is very rarely as interesting.

Raveneau

BURGUNDY

FROM SMALL BEGINNINGS THE RAVENEAU BROTHERS HAVE CONTINUED
TO PURSUE A FIERCELY HANDS-ON APPROACH, SO MUCH SO THAT THEIR
DOMAINE IS WIDELY ACKNOWLEDGED AS THE FINEST IN CHABLIS.

"Chablis is both a very old and a very young *vignoble*," says Bernard Raveneau. Before the phylloxera epidemic vineyards stretched all the way from Dijon to Sens and beyond, almost to the doors of Paris. The land was polycultural, but the wines of Chablis were well known, and attracted a premium. And communication with the capital was easy. But by the time the pestilence arrived in Chablis in 1893, rather later than elsewhere, a market decline had already set in. By this time, the railway had opened up the south of France, and the local wines just could not compete.

The next eighty years were years of severe depression. The Chablis vineyard contracted. As a result of the savage frost in 1945 not a single bottle of Chablis was produced that year. Old-timers remember skiing down the slope of the *grands crus* in 1961. In this vintage the area under vine for the whole of Chablis was a mere 350 hectares.

If one looks at Chablis in this context it is easy to understand why Bernard and Jean-Marie Raveneau's grandfather, Louis, who had inherited vines from *his* father, decided to sell them off in the 1950s. They were, simply put, unprofitable. The Raveneaus, of bourgeois origin, could think of better ways of making a living.

Louis's son, François, however, had other ideas. Firstly, he had married Andrée, sister of René Dauvissat (of today's Domaine René & Vincent Dauvissat). He got on well with his in-laws, Robert and Alice, and had inherited some vines in Les Clos and Les Forêts through his wife. François started building up his own estate. Land was cheap. Gradually throughout the 1960s and 1970s he acquired parcels of good vines, resulting in a domaine which today covers 7.8 hectares. He died in 2000 at the age of seventy-nine.

There is half a hectare of Les Clos, 0.75 hectares in Valmur, and 0.62 in Blanchots, all *grand cru*, plus twenty-seven hectares in Montée de Tonnerre just next door, 0.3 hectares in Chapelot, 1.5 in Butteaux, 0.4 in Vaillons, 0.4 in Montmains, and 0.6 in Les Forêts, all *premier cru*.

The Domaine Raveneau is today jointly run by Jean-Marie, born in 1955, who joined his father in 1979, and his elder brother Bernard, born in 1950, who spent fifteen years working with local merchants Régnard, and who joined the family business only in 1995.

OPPOSITE *Bottles maturing in the Raveneau cellar. These are among the longest-lasting of all Chablis*

"It all starts in the vineyard," say the Raveneaus. "The first essential is to keep the harvest under control. We haven't invented anything. Everyone could do the same." While freely admitting that in 2000, as a result of rain before the harvest and the huge *sortie*, they produced as much as 70 hl/ha, the Raveneaus prune and de-bud with the intention of yielding 45—50 ha/hl.

Raveneau is one of the rare Chablis domaines where everything, even the basic Chablis, is collected by hand. Why? It is a question of control, of being able to sort out the good fruit from the bad. Today more and more estates who possess *grands* and *premiers crus* have reverted to manual harvesting. Yet most still pick the lesser vineyards mechanically. Thereafter the fruit is crushed but not destemmed, pressed — since 2002 in a pneumatic apparatus — and allowed to settle overnight. Ten per cent is vinified in new wood, ten per cent in last year's wood, eight per cent in tank. After malolactic, the *cuvées* are blended and then stored in cask for a year before bottling.

So what is it that the Raveneau brothers do which others don't? Why is their wine (and those of their Dauvissat cousins, I have to add) so far superior and less ephemeral than most of the rest? "We have twice as many workers [six, including themselves] as other domaines of this size," they admit. So, I suggest, they can take more pains. The small size of the usual Raveneau crop leads to the fact that, since 1987, they have had to chaptalize only in 2000, 1997, 1993, and just a little in 1995. I am also sure that the hand-harvesting, and the fruit selection that comes with this, are paramount. You don't make first-division wine with second-division fruit.

And there has been a passing down, through the generations, of an *esprit de qualité*. "Not from the paternal side, but the maternal side. I didn't like my grandfather, Louis Raveneau," said Bernard. "And he didn't like me. But I had great respect for my mother's father, Robert Dauvissat. He had get up and go. He sold direct to the top Parisian restaurants long before anyone else. He was the first to experiment with different rootstocks." The bond between Jean-Marie and Bernard and René Dauvissat is still close.

Domaine de la Romanée-Conti

BURGUNDY

THE DOMAINE DE LA ROMANEE-CONTI HAS FOR GENERATIONS BEEN THE FINEST ESTATE IN BURGUNDY. IN TERMS OF *GRANDS CRUS* IT IS ALSO THE LARGEST, WITH AN UNPARALLELED GALAXY OF VINEYARDS.

The Domaine de la Romanée-Conti (DRC) owns the entirety of two *climats*, La Romanée-Conti and La Tâche. It possesses approximately half of Richebourg, over a third of Grands-Echézeaux, and one-seventh of Echézeaux, this last holding being in the *lieu-dit* Les Poulaillères, the best part of this large *grand cru*. It also used to "farm", but since 1988 has owned, the portion — over half of the appellation — of Domaine Marey-Monge's Romanée-St-Vivant. This makes the total Vosne-Romanée *grand cru* holding as follows:

	Hectares	Average age of vines
La Romanée-Conti	1.81	47 years
La Tâche	6.06	45 years
Richebourg	3.51	28 years
Grands-Echézeaux	3.53	45 years
Echézeaux	4.67	30 years
Romanée-St-Vivant	5.29	25 years

In addition, the domaine owns 0.68 hectares of Le Montrachet, 0.17 hectares of Bâtard, and about one hectare of communal Vosne. The last two are not sold under the domaine label but in bulk to local merchants, as is the produce of young vines on the more famous slopes.

The Abbé Courtepée in the eighteenth century, echoed by Camille Rodier in the twentieth, said of Vosne-Romanée, *"Il n'y a pas de vin commun"* — there are no common wines in the village. The wines were famous then, and are just as highly regarded now. The mixture of the right exposure, on a well-drained slope facing east or southeast, soil which is essentially an oolitic, iron-rich limestone on a base of marl, rock, and pebbles, and vines which lie approximately between 250 and 300 metres (984 feet) above sea level, sheltered from the west and north by the trees at the top of the slope, is as good as you can get. The *grand cru climats*, plumb in the middle of the slope, are the best of all, and DRC has the lion's share of these.

La Tâche lies between Les Malconsorts and La Grande Rue, 255–300 metres (837–984 feet) in altitude, steeper at the top, flatter at the bottom, but well drained nonetheless. It comprises a number of soil structures, with decomposed limestone of the Bathonian period at the top, thinly

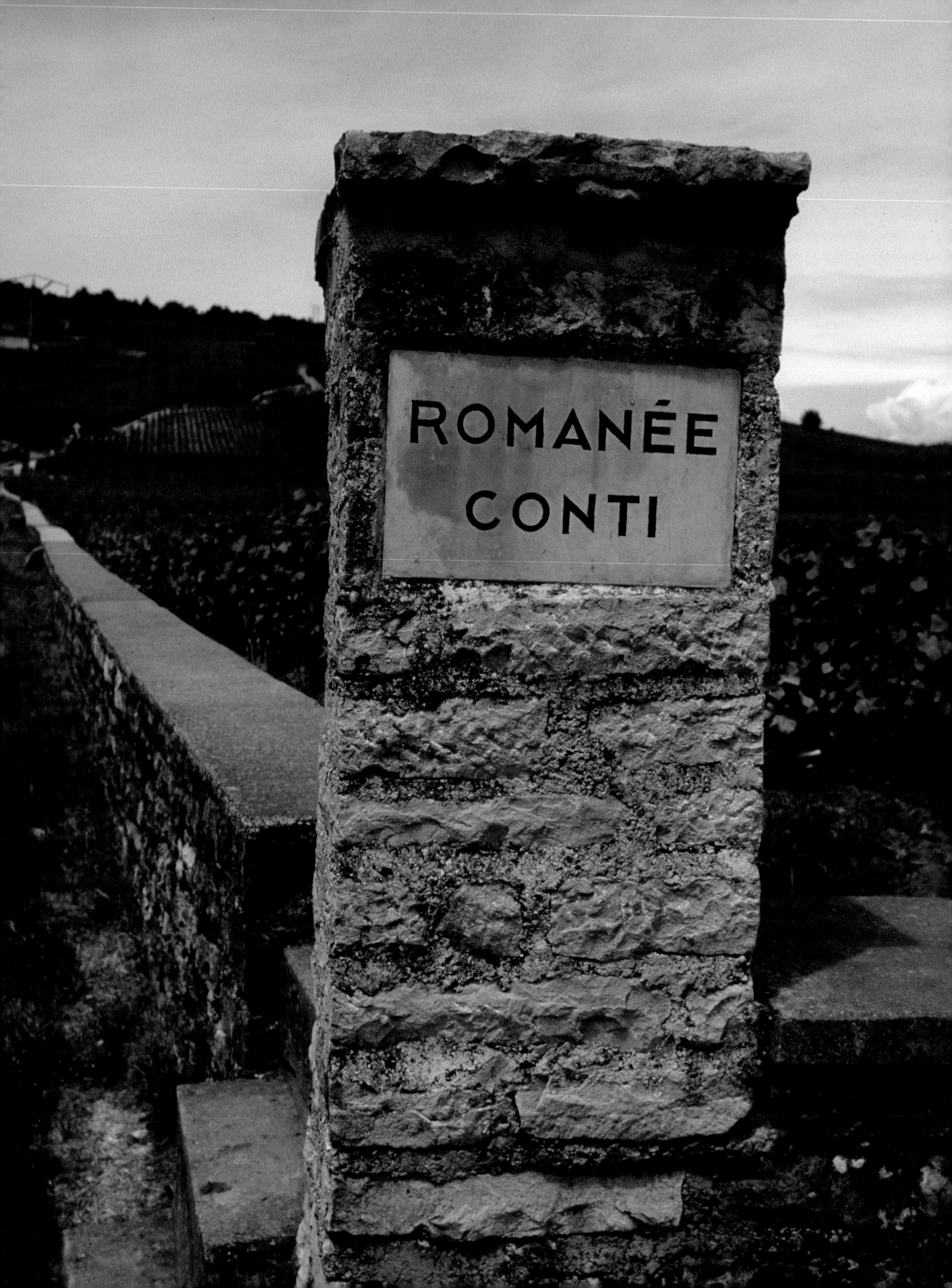
ROMANÉE
CONTI

covered by pebbles and limestone debris; deeper, richer, more clayey soil at the bottom of the slope, in parts mixed with fossilized oyster deposits. As with all the DRC vineyards, it is cultivated organically.

La Tâche is produced in the same way as the other DRC wines. The vineyard is densely planted, with 110 centimetres (43 inches) between the rows and eighty centimetres (31.5 inches) between the vines, making it 11,250 vines per hectare. Every year or two as the vines die, a small number are replaced, keeping the average age of the vineyard at forty-five years or more. Until the vines are at least ten years old, their fruit is vinified separately.

Severe pruning and de-budding keep the harvest low. It was less than 30 hl/ha in 2001, for instance. So green harvesting is unnecessary. What happens instead a week or so before the harvest begins is that a *passage de néttoyage* (cleaning) is undertaken. The team of workers go through the vines to reject anything sub-standard, including bunches which are backward in maturity, or incapable of ripening properly. This makes the picking easier.

The DRC tradition, abandoned by most, is to vinify with the stems. Another, where they were pioneers, is to sort out the fruit on its arrival at the winery. Everyone now has a *tapis de triage*. Few do not destem. The arguments against destemming are that the stems may not be as ripe as one would wish, imparting a green herbaceous taste, and even if they are ripe, they will interfere with the extraction of not only colour, but the fruit's freshness and purity, and the nobility of the grape tannins. The DRC argument is that the tannins which derive from the stems can be just as high in quality, that it gives the wine extra structure and staying power, that the stemmy taste will be absorbed during the ageing process, and that the wine becomes more complex.

After fermentation at temperatures of up to 32°C (90°F) and maceration for about two to three weeks, the wine is racked into new barrels from the forest of Tronçais in the Allier via François Frères in St-Romain. There it will stay, racked usually only once, until given a little fining with fresh, whisked-up egg whites after eighteen months or so. Six or so casks at a time the wines are assembled *sur colle*, allowed to rest, and then bottled in the domaine's specially produced, old-fashioned, heavy glass. They are then held for up to a year before release.

La Tâche is normally the fullest, most long-lasting, richest, and most concentrated of the DRC wines. The Romanée-Conti itself may be the most subtle, complex, and refined of the line-up. But La Tâche, with its extra power, can be equally as noble. According to a 1783 inventory, Louis XVI had some in the royal cellar. So should everyone.

champagne & alsace

Champagne is simply the world's greatest sparkling wine for depth, subtlety, and ability to age, while the wines of Alsace combine the remarkable, food-friendly nature of German varietals with a sizeable dose of French flair – here dry Rieslings rule supreme.

Krug

CHAMPAGNE

ARGUABLY THE GREATEST CHAMPAGNE HOUSE OF ALL, KRUG'S
REVERENCE FOR THE QUALITY OF GOOD WINES MEANS THAT
NOTHING IS HURRIED, LEAST OF ALL THE AGEING PROCESS.

There are some brand names — Rolls-Royce, Guerlain, Cartier — that are synonymous with the highest quality. Fashions may come and go, but certain names endure. To achieve this sort of recognition you need more than just a certain amount of dedication and expertise, and you certainly require something additional to a large advertising budget. You need a philosophy of excellence; one that is steeped in history and as firm and as unconditional as a rock. Ask anyone, "Who produces the best Champagne?" On everyone's list will be the House of Krug.

What is it about Krug which makes it such a good Champagne? What is the recipe for such quality? There is no magic formula, say the Krugs — the *encépagement* (blend) varies considerably from year to year, for instance — nor, necessarily, is there an unconditional adherence to old-fashioned methods. A blinkered attitude towards technological innovation is certainly not one of the ingredients.

In many ways, however, the approach is traditional. For a start every single drop of wine is fermented in casks of 205 litres, of which three per cent are renewed every vintage. A normal harvest for Krug will yield 3,000—3,500 casks of wine. One hundred of these will be vinified in new oak. They have occasionally experimented with fermenting in stainless steel, but always found the oak-fermented wine to be the more complex, the most aromatic. "For us," says Rémi Krug, currently at the helm with brother Henri, "vinification in oak is a determining factor of the quality of our wines."

Secondly, only the first pressing is used. The wine is fermented at 19—22°C (66—71°F), never filtered, and racked only by gravity. An impressive bank of reserve wines is held in stainless-steel tanks of 4,000-litre capacity and the Champagne is not put on the market for five years or more after bottling. For sales of about half a million bottles, a cellar of three million bottles — six years' worth — is stocked. Up to five years a wine can usefully feed off its lees, the Krugs will tell you, but after that they have little to add to the wine.

Krug does not produce a *cuvée de luxe*: "Our vintage wine is the best we can produce. Why dilute it by creaming off a theoretical five per cent?" This is not marketed until seven or eight years old — none of this regrettable rushing to be the first to get a new vintage into the shops

ABOVE *Champagne bottles on their pupitres in the Krug cellars*

before the wine has hardly settled down in bottle, let alone developed any depth and concentration. As I write, the 1990 is just about to be released: a magnificent wine which has still not reached its apogee.

But then what is the Krug Collection? These are wines from the Krug reserves, essentially exactly the same wines, but older. "I call it a second life," says Rémi. "Wines with the tertiary flavours of full maturity." They are old and rare, but vigorous and profound in flavour. Released in grudgingly small quantities, they are individually numbered and packed in single-bottle wooden cases. The current vintages available on the UK market start with the 1981 and go backwards. They will cost you in the region of about £250 a bottle.

One of the great Champagnes is Krug 1928. It is a wine which Rémi Krug, who started working for his family in 1965, has drunk often but in his youth, rather more often than you would expect even a young *champenois* to have done.

We go back to the early days of World War II. In those days the only market for vintage wine was Britain. All the 1928 had been sold via Krug's London agents to their customers. But by no means all had been shipped. Joseph Krug was therefore in a dilemma. This wine could be seized by the Germans as enemy property. His solution was to cancel the paid reserves, and to sell them to himself personally. Luckily he was rich enough to be able to write out what must have been a substantial cheque! The wines could be "hidden".

After hostilities ceased, the rightful British owners of the stocks of 1928 were asked whether they wanted the wine shipped. Many preferred to switch to a more recent vintage, for instance the 1937. Perforce, Joseph Krug remained the owner of the unwanted 1928. Well, if you've got it, he said, you might as well drink it. So at almost any excuse a bottle or two of Krug 1928 was popped by all the family. Joseph Krug lived to be 98. Towards the end of his life he enquired of his children how much 1928 remained. He then commanded them to cease opening any more bottles. "We'll save it all for my 100th birthday," he said. Sadly, this was not to occur. Happily for good friends of the Krugs, some stock still remains.

Pol Roger

CHAMPAGNE

THE FAMILY-OWNED HOUSE OF POL ROGER PRODUCES ONE OF THE
FINEST AND MOST RELIABLE RANGES OF CHAMPAGNE, WITH EXEMPLARY
CUVEES FROM NON-VINTAGE ALL THE WAY TO ITS PRESTIGE OFFERINGS.

Britain is one of France's leading export markets for Champagne, and for many Grand Marque houses this market dominates their export sales. Few, however, can be so embedded in the country as Pol Roger. No other has gone so far as to name its prestige brand after a British statesman — Sir Winston Churchill. Pol Roger is that brand. For quite a while, it has been one of my favourite Champagnes.

Pol Roger — Pol was his Christian name, a corruption of Paul perhaps — the son of Charles Jean Baptiste Roger, was born in Aÿ in 1831. His family, one can assume, were local tenant farmers or small businessmen. Certainly they owned no land in their own right. In 1849, after a brief apprenticeship with another Champagne house, Pol set up his own Champagne business at the youthful age of eighteen.

The Churchill connection begins with a lunch party given by the ambassadress Lady Diana Cooper at the British Embassy in Paris in November 1944. There Winston Churchill met Madame Odette Pol Roger, wife of Jacques, Pol Roger's grandson. Madame Pol Roger was *née* Wallace, one of three ravishingly beautiful daughters of General Wallace, known throughout society as the Wallace Collection! Winston, who like most sensible men was attracted to wit, intelligence, and beauty, particularly when combined in the one person, was entranced. They were firm friends for the rest of his life.

When Sir Winston died in 1965, the Pol Roger family paid him the highest tribute they could command. They bordered their label in black, in mourning for their English friend. Nineteen years later there came another accolade. The launch of a prestige brand: Cuvée Sir Winston Churchill. Appropriately the label is black, embossed with gold. The wine was launched at Blenheim Palace, Sir Winston's birthplace.

Pol Roger is one of the few large Champagne houses which is completely independent. Apart from a minimal percentage, the shareholding remains within the family. The company produces and sells about 1.3 million bottles of wine, seventy per cent of which is the famous White Foil NV and sixty per cent of which is exported. Current stocks are between six and seven million bottles, about 4.5 years' worth of sales. They own eighty-five hectares of land,

ABOVE *The impressive façade of
the Pol Roger château in Epernay*

ABOVE *The long steep ascent*
from the depths of the
Pol Roger cellars

which provides some sixty per cent of their wine requirements.

The cellars, largely constructed in the mid-nineteenth century, run for ten kilometres (6.2 miles) and are on three levels, the deepest of which is known as the *cave de prise de mousse* and is thirty-three metres (108.3 feet) below road level. As the name suggests, this is where the wine undergoes its second fermentation in bottle. The fact that this deep cave is at 9°C (48°F) or less, rather than a normal cellar temperature of 11–12°C (52–54°F), prolongs this fermentation and is one contributing factor to the quality and individual style of the wine and its particularly fine mousse. *Remuage* (turning the bottles on the pupitres) is entirely manual.

The Pol Roger range begins with its White Foil. This non-vintage blend is made from equal parts of each of the three Champagne grapes: Chardonnay, Pinot Noir, and Pinot Meunier. It is kept for four years before being released to the world, and is one of the best and most consistent on the market. On the palate it is fresh with a ripe acidity, and is a most appetising, stylish, more-ish glass of wine. Its impeccable mousse is a characteristic found in all Pol Roger Champagnes.

The Brut Vintage is currently a sixty : forty Pinot Noir/Chardonnay blend. While the family has gently lightened the style of Pol Roger over the years, it is still a Champagne on the full side, a wine of vigour as well as richness, with plenty of depth as well as balance. Sumptuous would be a good description.

Little seen in the UK, where naturally the Cuvée Winston Churchill takes pride of place, is Pol Roger's other prestige brand, the Réserve Spéciale PR. This wine was launched in the early 1990s and is a fifty : fifty Pinot Noir/Chardonnay blend. A really fine wine: the epitome of elegance.

And the Churchill itself? More masculine, more Pinot Noir; in a different way equally excellent. Drink the PR as an apéritif, the Churchill with food or after a meal. Either would be luxury; both would be a moment in paradise.

Louis Roederer

CHAMPAGNE

AN EVEN MORE PERFECTIONIST ATTITUDE THAN FOUND
ELSEWHERE AMONGST ITS PEERS MAKES ROEDERER ONE
OF THE TRULY GREAT CHAMPAGNE HOUSES.

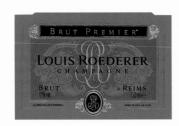

The reputation of Louis Roederer's Cristal speaks for itself. Less well known, perhaps, but equally worthy of recognition are Roederer's Brut Vintage and its non-vintage, Brut Premier. This is one of the greatest of all Champagne houses, one even more dedicated to the highest quality than most. Ask Jean-Claude Rouzaud, Roederer managing director, what is wrong with Champagne today, and he will answer quite simply: "Overproduction" before going on to say, "While there have been vintages recently such as 1982, 1989, 1990, and so on which might suggest that you can produce both volume and excellence, in fact the inverse proportionality will always prove true in the end. The absolute maximum yield is 12,000–13,000 kilograms per hectare — the latter usually the legal limit — but today we see growers achieving that while still leaving quantities of unpicked fruit in the vineyard. Most don't seem to care. Recently we sent round a letter to the forty-odd growers with whom we have special contracts. We offered an even larger bonus than we normally pay if they would agree to green harvest. Only two said 'yes.' Thank God we are eighty per cent self-sufficient from our own vineyards."

Why, you ask, remembering that the last seriously short Champagne vintage was back in 1985, is production so high these days? Is it just a result of growers' cynicism? "When I took over as *President Director General* in 1967," Rouzaud answers, "most vineyards held a significant percentage of unproductive vines. They don't any more. We have healthier, more disease-resistant clones. We don't plough the vineyards any more, so the vine's superficial roots proliferate, providing easy nourishment. The net result is that a bunch of grapes today yields 150 berries. Thirty-five years ago it was 100. I am convinced global warming has something to do with it. As a result, here at Roederer we never use anything but the *cuvée* [the first pressing]. We sell off or even throw away the *taille* [second and third pressings]."

This is a man of passion speaking. A perfectionist. Probably a hard taskmaster. "My team know well," he says with a smile, "that absolutely nothing is done at Roederer that I don't want to be done." This perfectionism runs all the way through the Roederer winery, from the vineyard to the cellars and its many procedures.

OPPOSITE *Hundreds of bottles of Roederer's prestige* cuvée, Cristal, *maturing gently in* pupitres

In 1967, Roederer owned 145 hectares, chiefly acquired in post-phylloxera times and in the 1920s by Rouzaud's ancestors, Louis-Victor and Léon Orly-Roederer. Today the figure is approaching 200 hectares and Roederer is continuing to buy. There are some 350 parcels throughout the main Champagne grape-growing regions: fifty hectares in the Montagne, fifty in the Valley, seventy-five in the Côte des Blancs, the rest elsewhere. The average vineyard rating is high: 97.5 per cent, where 100 per cent denotes *grand cru* status. There are press houses at four locations.

As well as relying on its growers under contract, Roederer has to search elsewhere for its requirements. It looks only in the Côte des Blancs for Chardonnay. You get the distinct feeling that Pinot Meunier is slightly looked down upon — none of the vintage wines contains a drop.

Roederer's wines normally do not undergo malolactic fermentation. The vintage wines are held five years before disgorging, the Cristal being manually disgorged on pupitres, the rest using *gyropalettes* (machine-controlled) — "No difference if properly done," says Jean-Claude Rouzaud — and the non-vintage three. Since 1998 this period for the Brut Premier has been deliberately extended. One aspect of perfectionism which has escaped them is the use of the crown cork for the entire range. Tastings I have done elsewhere leave me convinced that for quality vintage wines better results are achieved using real corks. Roederer currently does not accept this.

Apart from that, across the board from Blanc de Blancs to very stylish *rosés* produced by skin contact, quality is exemplary. They probably produce more vintage wine as a percentage turnover than any other Champagne house. You can do that only if the wines are good.

Trimbach

ALSACE

ELEVEN GENERATIONS OF TRIMBACHS HAVE WORKED THIS LAND. MUCH CAREFUL ATTENTION PRIOR TO HARVEST LEADS TO THE FAMILY WINERY'S SUPERLATIVE STYLE OF RESTRAINED OPULENCE AND SLEEK COMPLEXITY.

Below the church of Hunawihr, in the heart of Alsace, are the vines of the 1.25-hectare Clos Ste-Hune, part of the sixteen-hectare *grand cru* Rosacker. The soil of Clos Ste-Hune is a chalky limestone containing fossilized shells, deposited at the time when the land between the Vosges and the Black Forest collapsed and was inundated by sea. The locals call it *muschelkalk*.

The Clos Ste-Hune vineyard has belonged to the highly respected local firm of F.E. Trimbach for over two hundred years. The Trimbachs originated in the eponymous village in northwestern Switzerland, roughly equidistant between Berne, Lucerne, and Basle, and arrived in Alsace in 1574. In 1626 a wine firm was established, and it continues to this day, eleven generations later, still family owned.

RIGHT *Trimbach's cellars nestling among the buildings of Riquewihr*

LEFT *Riesling performs beautifully on the steep slopes of the Osterberg vineyard right behind the cellars of Trimbach*

Today the directors of the firm are Bernard, who is now retired, his younger brother Hubert, and Bernard's sons, Pierre and Jean. Pierre makes the wine, Hubert and Jean sell it.

The unpretentious Trimbach winery shelters under the vineyard of Osterberg just outside the village of Ribeauvillé on the road to Bergheim. The Trimbachs own a good slice of the Osterberg, planted with Riesling and from which comes another of the jewels of the portfolio, the Cuvée Frédéric Emile, as well as land in the nearby Trottacker vineyard, from whence comes their top Gewurztraminer, named after the local *seigneurs* of the late Middle Ages, the Seigneurs de Ribeaupierre. In total the family owns thirty hectares of land, which together with a further eighty under long-term contract with other local growers gives a production of one million bottles a year. Three-quarters is exported.

The Trimbach wines are forthright, austere, and at their best magnificent. Vinification is in stainless steel or large old wooden *foudres,* and takes place over an extended period at a cool temperature. The malolactic fermentation is not always proceeded with. The result is something in complete contrast to the softer, plumper, more forthcoming examples produced by their friendly rivals Hugel in Riquewihr. Trimbach wines are reserved, steely, and elegant. They are my style of Alsace.

The Clos Ste-Hune is made in broadly the same way as the rest of the Trimbach range. There is no magic ingredient. The vineyard is made up of vines of a medium average age — twenty-five years — which are severely pruned, and the crop is further ruthlessly cut down later in the season by thinning out every third or fourth bunch on the most vigorous vines. The average yield is around 50 hl/ha rather than the 70 or 80 elsewhere.

While a few vines are occasionally left to mature longer to make a little Vendange Tardive — up to 1989 the quantities were very small, and the wine was kept for private consumption, but more is made and marketed today — the vineyard is normally cleared when the grapes reach a potential alcohol of 12.5 degrees or so and is harvested by a series of *passages* through the vines. Each bunch is therefore collected at an optimum state of ripeness. The wine is bottled the following April and not released for a further five years. It would be infanticide for it to be consumed too young! Only about 8,000 bottles are produced each year.

And the wine? It is the most glorious expression of the noble Riesling grape. Dry but rich and concentrated; restrained but opulent; positively balanced and definitely fruity, with an elegance, a subtlety, and a complexity which is — in the case of the 1990 — quite brilliant: a dream of a wine. Compared with other Rieslings, the Cuvée Frédéric Emile for example, it is extremely steely and racy. It is a lithe wine; as streamlined as a racehorse, as lean and aloof as a mannequin. Clos Ste-Hune is not cheap. But it is worth every penny.

loire

France's longest river has much to fascinate the wine lover, from the exquisite wines of Pouilly and Sancerre, via the eloquent Chenin Blancs of Touraine and Anjou, to its increasingly fine roster of reds.

Florent Baumard

LOIRE

WITH VINEYARDS IN A VARIETY OF SUPERB LOCATIONS AND THE SKILLS AND PATIENCE TO MAKE TOP CHENIN-BASED WINES, BOTH SWEET AND DRY, BAUMARD IS THE LEADING DOMAINE IN THE WESTERN ANJOU.

One of the larger and most versatile domaines of the Anjou is that of the Baumards, today managed by the handsome, youthful, forty-year-old Florent Baumard. With a base in Rochefort and a total of thirty-five hectares, the Domaine des Baumard has a foot on either side of the river Loire, being major owners both in Quarts de Chaume and Savennières.

We drive from Rochefort to the Quarts de Chaume, one of the most prized jewels in the sweet wine crown of Coteaux du Layon. The distance is hardly three kilometres (1.9 miles), yet even in the depths of winter you feel you have passed a barrier into a softer, warmer climate. Above the stream of the Layon the slopes are precipitous. Each vine is supported

RIGHT *The modest entrance to the Domaine des Baumard winery in Rochefort*

by its own stake. Each row occupies a single terrace. I am reminded of Côte-Rôtie. Here the soil is gritty schist over schistous rock containing veins of quartz.

Just as the Domaine des Baumard possesses the western edge of the Quarts de Chaumes, so is their holding in Savennières on the oriental edge of a butterfly-shaped vineyard — hence the name Papillon — in a north-south steep-sided narrow gorge above the village of Savennières. The soil structure here is more complex. Volcanic in origin, it consists of a thick layer of loess mixed with a peculiarly coloured, blue-violet schist with veins of sandstone and granite. Beneath this is schistous rock. In the Baumard Savennières vineyard there is a lot of quartz.

All three vineyards are picked by *passages*: hand-harvested as a result of three, four, or more visits to each row of vines. "The quality and the timing of the harvest are crucial," says Florent. In the Savennières he aims to produce 50 hl/ha, in the Quarts de Chaume less than the average, which is 22 hl/ha, in the Clos de Ste-Catherine at Rochefort only marginally more. There is a triage in the vineyard, no destemming, and a very careful pressing using pneumatic machines. "The care you take with the pressing is all important," says Florent. "With the sweet wines we press three times. The first gives us a juice with higher acidity, less richness. The second gives us the lusciousness and the third the backbone: this *cuvée* contains more tannin." When Florent's father Jean started, he fermented in oak barrels. Now there are a number of small stainless-steel vats, one for every pressing.

Savennières can be sweet or dry, although these days most is made dry. Over the years, Florent has experimented with oak barrels for the maturing of his Savennières, but doesn't consider this adds anything. In the 1950s and 1960s Jean was one of the first to investigate the effects of malolactic fermentation. Today they leave it to nature. The wine is racked to

eliminate the gross lees. There is occasional *bâtonnage*, and then, after a year, it is time to bottle the Savennières.

As well as the Clos du Papillon and the basic Domaine des Baumard, a rich rather than sweet Savennières called Trie Spéciale is produced from late-harvested grapes in suitable vintages such as 2000, 1997, 1995, 1990, and 1989. This must be the modern-day equivalent of the top Savennières of the past. Good as the Clos du Papillon usually is, this is worth the premium, in my view.

In addition to the single-vineyard Clos de Ste-Catherine, the Domaine des Baumard offers, of course, other Coteaux du Layons. There is Carte d'Or, and a Cuvée Ancienne de Jean Baumard. But the next best to the Catherine in my view has to be the Cuvée Le Paon.

When I first began to discover the Baumard wines in the early 1970s, they often suffered from an excess of built-in sulphur. Sulphur and Chenin Blanc, dry or sweet, was an even worse mixture than sulphur and other grape varieties such as Chardonnay. Today the levels are rather less. The wines are much cleaner.

What else has Florent done since he took over in 1996? He thinks for a minute. "I found that I had very much the same taste as Papa. We'd choose the same wines with the same dish in restaurants but on separate occasions. I haven't felt I needed to make any major alterations. So there's really been little to do except to refine and update. I am proud of what my father achieved. I am proud to be his successor."

Clos Rougeard

LOIRE

SAUMUR-CHAMPIGNY IS NOT A PARTICULARLY WELL-REPUTED RED WINE
LOIRE APPELLATION, BUT THE FOUCAULT BROTHERS PRODUCE SOME
OF THE BEST RED WINES OF THE ENTIRE LOIRE REGION.

Every so often for reasons which at first are difficult to explain, you come across someone in a relatively minor appellation who produces extraordinarily good wine. Even when you get there, lured by magnificent bottles you have sampled elsewhere, you find it hard to answer the basic question: why are these so good? What is it about this particular domaine which makes it so special? What do they have, in terms of terroir, and what is it that they do with it that produces such excitement?

One such is the Saumur-Champigny domaine of the brothers Charlie and Nady Foucault. This is located at Chacé, a rather charmless village in the middle of an equally unprepossessing plateau south of Saumur itself.

Charlie and his younger brother Nady are both in their early fifties. The duties at this ten-hectare estate are shared between them, as they have been since they took over in 1969, although the latter is also responsible for the commercial side.

The headquarters of the Clos Rougeard lie in the middle of the village of Chacé. A courtyard provides access to a ramshackle collection of modest and dilapidated farmhouses and barns beneath which is a rabbit warren of galleries and cellars hacked out of the underlying *tuffeau*, the limestone base rock of the Saumur-Champigny appellation. Behind this is the one-hectare vineyard of the estate's best wine: Le Bourg. The vines here are seventy years old. The clayey surface soil is a mere twenty centimetres (7.8 inches) deep. Elsewhere, on slightly better-drained, more sandy surface soil is the three-hectare, forty-five-year-old vineyard of Les Poyeux.

The remaining parcels, which produce the basic Saumur-Champigny, a little dry Saumur Blanc, and, when conditions allow, some sweeter Coteau de Saumur, lie scattered throughout the rest of the appellation.

The whole setup is artisanal in the extreme, old fashioned in the very best sense. The vineyard is ploughed. No herbicides or artificial fertilizers have ever been used. Yields are naturally very low. The fruit is completely destemmed, with a triage both before the harvest and afterwards. There is never any chaptalization or acidification, and the wines are fermented slowly, over as long as six weeks, at temperatures which can rise to 33°C (91°F), with both

ABOVE *The Clos Rougeard*
cellar has been hacked out of
the rock under the Foucault's
house in Chacé

pumping over and treading down, by feet, naturally, not machine. The *vin de presse* is not used, and the wines undergo malolactic fermentation in barrel. The Bourg is matured in new wood, the Poyeux in one-year-old oak and the generic in older wood. Bottling takes place without fining or filtration after eighteen months to two years.

Mention Saumur–Champigny to most people and they will come up with a memory of a wine rather lighter than Chinon or Bourgueil, perhaps not even aged in oak, probably best drunk slightly chilled, like Beaujolais; a wine of upfront fruit which is usually at its best young, say three years after the vintage.

This is precisely what most Saumur–Champignys are like. They represent the most stylish examples of Anjou's Cabernet Franc reds. But just as there are now one or two Anjou *villages* made for laying down, and just as, in the reverse sense, most Chinon producers offer a *primeur cuvée* from their lesser soils and younger vines, so is there now a new generation of Saumur–Champigny reds. The Foucault brothers are in the vanguard of this new trend. So far they have no close rivals.

These are substantial wines, but without over-extraction. They are oaky, but not exaggeratedly so. They have remarkably sophisticated tannins. They have excellent grip and very fine, very concentrated fruit. They are pure, harmonious, and elegant. All this adds up to a wine which would put much of Bordeaux to shame, as well as something which stands as high as any other red wine domaine in the Loire Valley. Moreover the Clos Rougeard wines are surprisingly fine in the lesser vintages.

I can only conclude that there is obviously more to this Saumur–Champigny appellation than we thought.

Coulée de Serrant

THE GRAND CLOS OF THE COULEE DE SERRANT IS HOME TO THE WORLD'S FINEST DRY WINE MADE FROM THE FICKLE CHENIN GRAPE. IS IT PURE COINCIDENCE THAT ITS CREATOR IS A LEADING BIODYNAMICS PIONEER?

CLOS
DE LA
Coulée de Serrant
APPELLATION SAVENNIÈRES-COULÉE DE SERRANT CONTRÔLÉE

2002

Nicolas JOLY, Propriétaire-Viticulteur
au CLOS DE LA COULÉE DE SERRANT - 49170 SAVENNIÈRES
Mise en bouteilles au Château
PRODUCT OF FRANCE WHITE WINE NET CONTENTS : 750 ML ALC.: 14%/VOL

The vineyards of Coulée de Serrant and La Roche aux Moines lie at the northeastern end of the Savennières appellation between the villages of Epiré and Savennières. Both are in little side valleys to the Loire itself, and, as the Loire is flowing roughly southwest here, both have an exposure which is practically due south. The vines are protected from the wind, and enjoy full sun from dawn to dusk. The land rises sharply from the river, and still to this day is too steep to allow full mechanical cultivation. Erosion, too, can be a problem.

The soil is volcanic in origin, and consists of a thin layer of loess, mixed with a peculiarly coloured blue-violet schist, with veins of sandstone and granite. This sits on a more solid schistous base which, even in the hottest summers, retains enough humidity to succour the vines. The colour of stones is, as far as I know, unique to Savennières; certainly I have not met their like in any other vine-growing area.

The domaine consists of seven hectares of Coulée de Serrant, a separate sub-division of the Savennières appellation which is exclusive to the Joly family, headed these days by Nicolas Joly. Four hectares, the prime site, is a walled vineyard known as the Grand Clos. Then there is the Clos du Château, nearer the ruined tower, and the Plantes. In the vineyard of La Roche aux Moines, the Jolys have a further three hectares, bottled as Clos de la Bergerie, and there are an additional three hectares of Savennières, including the extremely steep vineyard of Becherelle, planted by Joly in 1985.

It was in 1981 that Joly stumbled on the theory of Biodynamic agriculture, in the form of a book by the Austrian philosopher Rudolf Steiner. "I took the book on a skiing holiday. It changed my life." Coulée de Serrant went completely Biodynamic in 1985. It was

CHATEAU
DE
LA ROCHE AUX MOINES
COULÉE DE SERRANT

RIGHT *Joly's Clos de la Bergerie wine comes from the La Roche aux Moines vineyard, first planted in the twelfth century in the tiny Coulée de Serrant appellation*

ABOVE *The prime Coulée de Serrant site was an ancient monastic vineyard. It slopes down towards the Joly family's Château de la Roche aux Moines*

a long-term process, though. Not until 1993, in my view, did Joly start to produce really fine wine. The 1988, 1989, and 1990 — all very good vintages for the area — were, and still are, hard and charmless, and over-sulphured to boot.

Biodynamics suggests that vines which are in a natural equilibrium with their environment will be healthy vines, better able to withstand adversity. But the vines are not left entirely alone to cope with the depredations of bugs and pests such as red spiders. Though Joly feels the presence of red spiders is not a real problem for healthy vines, he has nevertheless countered this arthropod by breeding a predator in his neighbouring orchard.

Other treatments are homeopathic. Why arsenic, which is fatal to plants as well as humans at a ten per cent solution, should be beneficial in a one part per 100 million dilution, when the "magic ingredient" cannot be chemically analyzed as being present, according to scientists, we do not understand. Joly employs a nettle infusion against snails and other parasites and to keep the sap circulating during a drought, and horsetail against cryptogamic diseases. Yarrow, camomile, oak, dandelion, and valerian are also used.

ABOVE *Many Biodynamic vineyards like those of Nicolas Joly at Coulée de Serrant have reverted to the use of horses for ploughing*

Moreover, and this is where Joly's Biodynamic methods begin to cross over the border from what the normal healthy sceptic would accept to what he would decry, the work cycle is run according to the stars. "Look," says Joly, "We know the moon influences the earth, tides, barometric pressure. Well, experiments in Germany have shown that plants can anticipate a solar eclipse twenty-four hours in advance.

"The position of the sun as well as that of the moon plays a part. As the sun passes through different constellations it produces four recurring types of influence which favour either the growth of leaves (water signs: Cancer, Scorpio, Pisces — this period is particularly favourable to leaf vegetables), the growth of roots (earth signs: Taurus, Capricorn, Virgo — favourable to root vegetables), the growth of flowers (air signs: Gemini, Libra, Aquarius), or the growth of fruit (fire signs: Aries, Sagittarius, Leo). The four elements are present: earth, air, fire, and water. Of course, it is the fire sign dates which are of importance in vine growing.

"Each of these periods has its own qualities, thus weeding under the influence of Leo (which stimulates reproduction in Biodynamic soil) will lead to a considerable increase in the size of grape pips, thus increasing natural tannins and making the modern practice of using new casks each year unnecessary. These rhythms were instinctively known by our ancestors. They would only plant or work the wine in the cellar at very precise times. Why ignore the influences and natural growth factors?"

Coulée de Serrant is a wine which requires long ageing. When young the acidity is dominant, and when recently bottled — even as long as five or six years later — the wine is lumpy and adolescent. It really needs a decade in most vintages. Then, and not until then, does the potentiality, seen in cask in the spring after the vintage, become actuality.

This Savennières is an austere wine, at its best with food; in good years it is certainly very distinguished; firm, full-bodied, ripe, complex, with a flowery, greengagey, Victoria plum character with nuances of honey, honeysuckle, and lime blossom. It is not, perhaps, sometimes, a very charming wine, and in the lesser vintages it can be a bit four-square. But at its best it can be magnificent. Moreover, as can be seen from the wines since 1993, Nicolas Joly's Biodynamic methods really do seem to work. Coulée de Serrant has become more noble, more intensely flavoured and more complex over the last decade. It hardly has to be said that it has become more individual.

Couly-Dutheil

LOIRE

IN MAKING CLOS DE L'ECHO, THE LOIRE'S FINEST RED WINE, THE COULY FAMILY BREAKS MANY CONVENTIONS IN ITS QUEST TO PRODUCE A RICH YET SUCCULENT *VIN DE GARDE* FROM THE CABERNET FRANC GRAPE.

If you stand among the vines on the plateau next to the fortress of Chinon, face the château and shout, your voice will bounce back off the buttressed stone wall of this famous monument. You are standing in the aptly named Clos de l'Echo, a seventeen-hectare vineyard which produces the greatest red wine of the Loire Valley.

I well remember when I first sampled the wine. It was the early 1970s and I was on my first trip to buy the wines of the Loire. At Les Rosiers, on the main road between Saumur and Angers, there was a Michelin-starred restaurant called Jeanne de Laval with a few bedrooms. It still exists, and it still has a star. On my first visit, having spent the best part of ten days working hard, I decided I deserved a good bottle of something. At the suggestion of the sommelier this turned out to be the Clos de l'Echo 1964. This was, and still is, a *grand vin*. I rang the Coulys the following morning to arrange a visit.

The estate is now run by brothers Jacques and Pierre, sons of founders René Couly and his wife, Madeleine Dutheil, with the next generation, Bertrand, taking the role of cellar master. The soil of the Clos de l'Echo is clay or clayey limestone containing quartz pebbles. The vineyard, gently facing south, lies on the highest point of Chinon, ideally exposed. Here the vines are planted one metre (3.3 feet) apart in rows two metres wide, with the space between alternately ploughed and grassed. Pruning is to five buds on a single cane, with the aim of producing 42 hl/ha.

"In the run-up to the harvest", explains Jacques Couly, "we take regular samples from all the different plots in the vineyard to measure precisely how the maturation is progressing. From this we produce a picking plan of campaign so we can attack every vine at its optimum. There is a triage both in the vineyards and on arrival at the winery — rebuilt in 1989 on three storeys, and working as much as possible by gravity — before a very gentle destemming. We want to vinify with as much whole berries as possible at the beginning in order to preserve the fruit and prevent oxidation. Each parcel is vinified separately."

While some of the lighter Chinon *cuvées* are cold-soaked at the start, the reverse happens for the Clos de l'Echo. The must is warmed to 20°C (68°F) so that the indigenous yeasts can

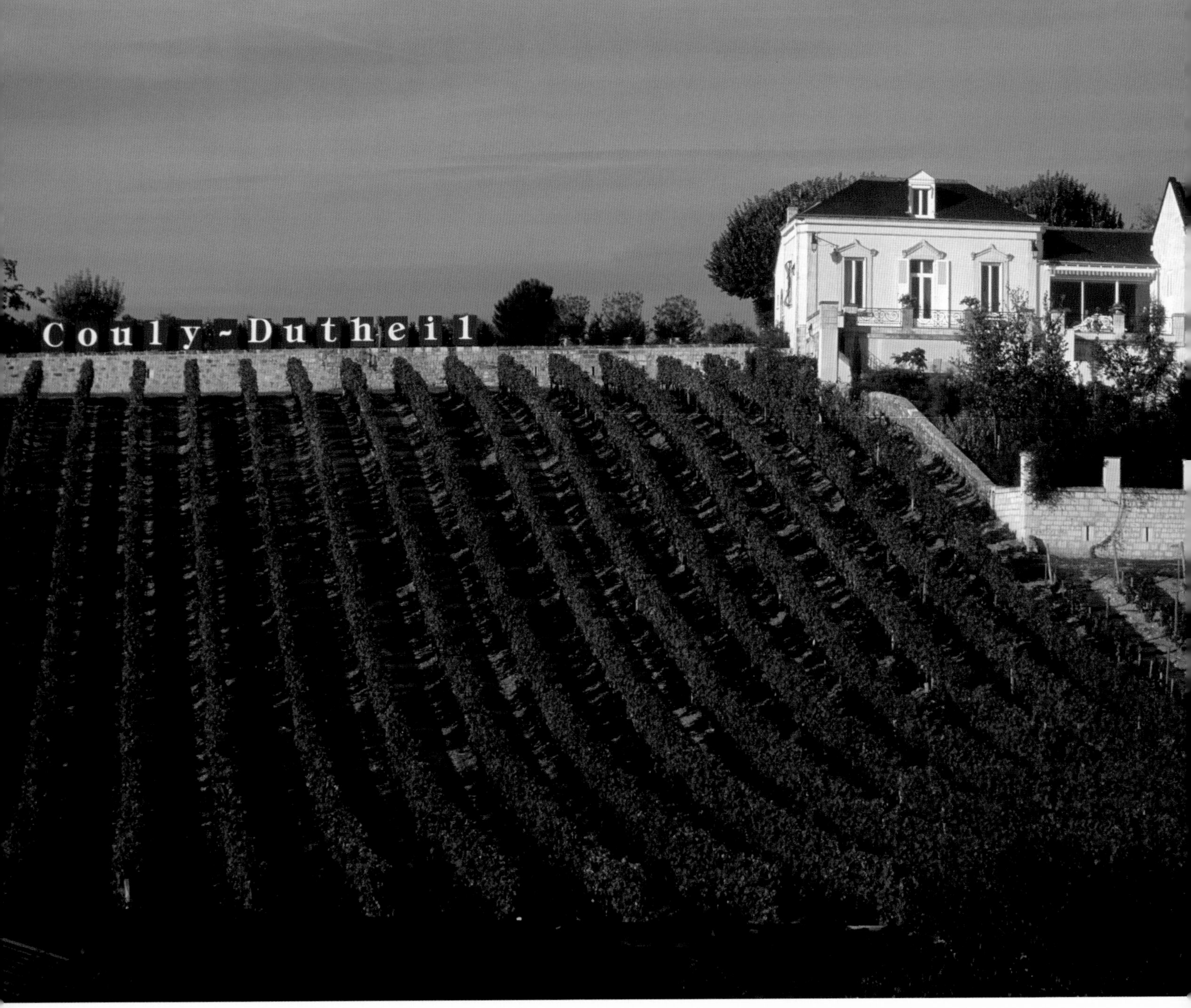
Couly-Dutheil

multiply quickly. "We want the fermentation to get under way as quickly as possible," says Bertrand. There is a very gentle mechanical *pigeage*, micro-oxygenation rather than lots of pumping over. "This preserves the fruit and oxidizes less, and in some years the fermentation temperature of 28°C (82°F) is raised to 32°C (90°F) at the end of the three- to five-week maceration in order to maximize the colour.

"The riper and richer the wine, the less new oak," is Bertrand's view. "So there is usually twenty per cent new, and in these casks the malolactic will take place. Clos de l'Echo is bottled after eighteen months."

Clos de l'Echo is of course not the only wine the firm of Couly-Dutheil produces. In all it now owns or leases 100 hectares, and has expanded from Chinon into Bourgueil (Château La Minière), St-Nicolas de Bourgueil, and Saumur-Champigny.

The second-best wine in the portfolio is the Clos de l'Olive, once owned by the Baron Charles de l'Olive-Noiré, conqueror of Guadeloupe in the seventeenth century. Other site-specific Chinons are the Domaine René Couly and La Diligence, while since 1995 a super-*cuvée* called Crescendo has been produced from the Clos de l'Echo in the best vintages.

ABOVE *The atmospheric entrance to the extensive Couly-Dutheil cellars in the heart of Chinon*

LEFT *The remarkable Clos de l'Echo vineyard lies on the highest point of Chinon and faces south, providing an excellent microclimate for its vines*

The red wines of the Loire have changed for the better over the last thirty years or so. In the past it was only in exceptional vintages such as 1947 and 1959 that you had wines with enough tannins which lasted and did not go stringy. The Coulys have been in the forefront of this progress. The Clos de l'Echo is a splendid example of a wine which is both succulent and a *vin de garde*.

No one who comes within ten kilometres (6.2 miles) of the beautiful township of Chinon, perched as it is on the Loire River, can fail to be reminded of sixteenth-century novelist François Rabelais's famous description of the wine as being like taffeta. With a mature bottle of Clos de l'Echo one can see what he was on about. Moreover, legend has it that the great man once owned the Clos himself.

Didier Dagueneau

LOIRE

THE WILD MAN OF POUILLY-FUME IS ALSO ONE OF ITS MOST PASSIONATE
ADVOCATES, ADDING NEW DIMENSIONS TO SAUVIGNON BLANC WITH HIS
USE OF WOOD AND INTIMATE UNDERSTANDING OF THE LOCAL TERROIR.

The moment you first catch sight of him you realize that Didier Dagueneau is no ordinary
vigneron. With his abundant red hair and beard, neither of which seem ever to have seen a
brush or comb, he looks like a combination of a tramp, a Viking, and a Celtic aboriginal.

Listening to him speak about wine will further confirm this view. All good winemakers
are passionate. Passion is an integral part of genius. But most have learned that it is wise to
be discreet at times. Dagueneau used to be the opposite of discreet.

Over the years since I first met him he has mellowed. "I've made a lot of mistakes in the
twenty years I have been making wine," he says. "And I am still learning. I screwed up the
1995 and 1996 vintages because I thought I could get away with low sulphur levels which
turned out to be too minimal. I tried Biodynamism, but then I got stuffed with mildew and
oidium. The only treatments allowed were too violent for the vines. As I get older the only
thing I am certain of is that I am less certain about things." This from the man who has almost
singlehandedly proved that new oak and the Sauvignon Blanc grape can coexist in harmony;
and who has demonstrated that this combination can produce great wines.

Since 1985 Dagueneau has steadily built up his domaine as well as exchanging parcels in
order to have more and more land containing quartz (silex), which is the soil round the back
of the Dagueneau home and winery. He now has eleven hectares. What is so special about
silex? I ask. "It is a much younger soil," says Dagueneau. "It dates from the Cretaceous era,
not the Jurassic such as soils which are Oxfordian (the oldest), Kimmeridgean, or Portlandian.
Silex soils are much poorer and less productive.

"We now harvest two weeks earlier than we did twenty years ago," he adds. "We used to
begin on 10th October, now it is 25th September. This is not necessarily a good thing. We may
harvest in better conditions, but the fruit has had two weeks less gestation."

Keeping the harvest down is today's major viticultural problem. "Viticulture is very
complex. There are no rules," Dagueneau says. "In some cases I plough the vines. In others
I don't. In some vintages you can make 60 hl/ha and produce fine wine. In others even 45
hl/ha is too much. I aim for 45. Even with my prices I can't afford to go down to 35." The

legal limit by the way is 72 hl/ha. Dagueneau was the first in his region to reduce the harvest seriously and deliberately.

"In order to make great wine one must get to grips with all the parameters: soil, density of planting, rootstock [he likes *Riparia Gloire* especially], pruning, de-budding, the amount of vegetation… The grapes must be ripe and healthy but full of flavour. Not exactly the same thing. If they are too healthy they have less taste. So we must go to the extreme limit of ripeness — almost at but not quite, the point of overripeness. So there are two, sometimes three *passages* through the vineyard."

There is a *triage* in the vines followed by a further sorting in the winery, before the fruit is destemmed. Dagueneau has tried pre-fermentation maceration (skin contact) to add an extra dimension. But he has found that with his yields the fruit was so ripe it was unnecessary. Equally because of the severe winter pruning and subsequent de-budding where necessary, he has not had to green harvest, nor to chaptalize.

Once fermented (there is of course no malolactic fermentation, Dagueneau does not want to diminish the wine's acidity), the wine is left on its fine lees with *bâtonnage* (stirring) until September. The wine is then racked into tanks to await bottling sometime during the winter. Dagueneau's grandfather stirred up the lees, bottled late, and had a cold cellar too, he says.

The Dagueneau range, at present, consists of four wines. In ascending order of quality and price they are: Les Chailloux, Pur Sang, Le Buisson Renard (from a separate plot of land), and Le Silex. Le Silex is probably the best Sauvignon-Blanc-based wine in the world.

RIGHT *The vineyards of Pouilly-Fumé with the church of St-Andelain in the distance*

Philippe Foreau

LOIRE

WITH A FIERCE RESPECT FOR THE LAND AND LITTLE IF ANY INTERFERENCE IN THE WINERY, PHILIPPE FOREAU'S CLOS NAUDIN PRODUCES SOME OF THE FINEST VOUVRAYS, ACROSS THE RANGE FROM *SEC* TO THE RARE *DOUX*.

"Of the 2,100 or so hectares of *appellation contrôlée* Vouvray," says Philippe Foreau, "only about 900 are capable of producing good still wine, and of this only 400 have the potential to make fine wine." Most of the locals realize this: seventy per cent of the Vouvray harvest is picked by machine all in one go, and becomes sparkling wine. This is the destination for anything Foreau picks which has less than a potential alcohol of 12 degrees.

"It is a question of terroir, of course," he says. "The best Vouvray soils are the slopes closest to the Loire where the composition is heavy clay mixed with quartz pebbles [silex] below which is the limestone rock out of which the locals have quarried the stone for the building of Vouvray and elsewhere. Further back from the river the clay is less profound, the exposition less fine, and the wines have less character. Even near to the river if there is not enough clay the wines are too ephemeral and lack elegance as well as depth. But paradoxically if you don't have enough silex the wines are also banal. The clay and the silex must be in equilibrium."

Here is a perfectionist speaking; a man with a horror of the standardization of the wines of today and nothing but contempt for those who do not have any respect for their land, or indeed the character of the vintage. "My reproach to some of my neighbours", says Foreau "is that most of the Vouvrays they produce are charming but flabby. They all taste the same. They have no energy. They cannot age."

Respect for the soil is a recurring Foreau *motif*. He is adamantly against herbicides, any systemic preparations, and even the planting of grass between the vines. "If one ploughs the land one gets better acidities. It's a rule." The vines are planted one metre (3.3 feet) apart, the rows 1.5 metres (5 feet) apart, and they are trained to a sort of two-dimensional *gobelet en éventail* (spur pruning in a fan- rather than bush-shape), and severely pruned to keep the yield to 35 hl/ha. Most of the domaine, certainly the best parcels, lies in a *lieu-dit* called Les Perruches, which is just above the house. Domaine Huët, a near neighbour and friendly rival, has its Le Mont in this sector too.

Picking of course is by *triage*, from mid-October well into November. The incidence of noble rot is less in Vouvray than in the Coteaux du Layon, hence the rarity of *doux* and indeed the

LEFT *The Clos Naudin cellar carved deep into the tuffeau rock under the vineyards*

relative infrequency by Layon standards of *moelleux* — only two or three times a decade.

"The Vouvray fruit concentrates as much by evaporation as by the attack of botrytis. The time of the harvesting is absolutely crucial," says Foreau, "as is of course the immediate elimination in the vineyard of anything sub-standard. Under a potential alcohol of 12 degrees, as I have said, the fruit is destined for sparkling wine. From 12—13.5 degrees it is made into *sec. Demi-sec* is from grapes which measure 13.5 degrees or more. If they reach 16 we can make *moelleux*. But of course the accompanying acidities are of vital importance."

The fruit is not destemmed, the stems aiding the pressing process, using a pneumatic machine. There is never any chaptalization, acidification, or added yeasts ("the vintage must be allowed to speak for itself"). And the wines are fermented — at cold temperatures, taking several months — and stored in old wood. Foreau says that the combination of new wood and the Chenin grape would be catastrophic. "The osmosis would be a disaster even with a long *élevage.*" And he bottles early to preserve the freshness and the fruit, before the following summer. In 2003, he says, we have three new barrels out of 100 in the cellar."

I ask him about malolactic fermentation (converting malic acid to lactic acid to soften acidity) for the *sec* wines (sweet wines never undergo malolactic). The answer is a withering look. Possibly, he acknowledges, for the cheap *vin de l'année* wines. "But if you allow malo to take place you emasculate the wine. It won't last. It won't be typical Vouvray. High acidities are essential."

"Each wine carries a message," says Foreau. "Vouvray is an old-established *vignoble*. So it has expanded by less than others elsewhere. At Foreau we are not big enough to produce a number of separate *lieu-dit* wines. The quantities would be too small to work with." But he'd like to see more growers isolating more high-quality *lieu-dit* wine from prime sites.

What I admire about Foreau's wines is that they are very pure, totally individual. Whether *sec, demi-sec,* or *moelleux,* each vintage radiates its own personality. They are both delicate and powerfully intense in flavour ("I don't like monsters," says Philippe. "I am after finesse.") And they last forever.

Thirty-five or more years ago, when I first began to visit the Foreau domaine, it was Philippe's father André who was the man in charge. Somewhat shy, and certainly diffident, he seemed rather bemused by the attention his wines were beginning to attract, and by the fact that some English foreigner had gone out of his way to pay him a visit. It was June, and we sat out in the shade of a venerable magnolia tree in his courtyard. No tasting ever seemed to have been planned. From time to time he would disappear into the murky tunnels of his cellar to emerge after a while with another couple of increasingly venerable and sweet, not to say rare, bottles. I learned to have patience. By and by he would become more relaxed and more articulate — and more expansive in his generosity. Thus it was that I tasted the fabled 1947, the finest vintage in living memory for sweet Loire wines.

Huët

LOIRE

THE BIODYNAMIC HUET ESTATE COMPRISES THREE KEY TERROIRS WITH CLEARLY IDENTIFIABLE PERSONALITIES. RUN BY NOEL PINGUET, IT IS JUSTLY REGARDED AS THE LEADING PROPERTY IN THE VOUVRAY REGION.

As three of the greatest *lieux-dits* in Vouvray belong to the same estate, and as this same estate is generally recognized as producing the finest wines of the appellation, you might imagine it to be of long standing, to have been passed down from father to son over the generations since the time of Napoleon at the very least. It is not as if Vouvray were a new *vignoble*. Wine has been produced here since the establishment of the Monastery of Marmoutier by St-Martin in AD 372.

But not so. The Huët domaine is relatively recent and was built up by the late Gaston Huët following the Second World War.

His son-in-law, Noël Pinguet, who has been in charge since 1971, will continue to run the estate following its recent sale to Anthony Huang, a Filipino-American financier, and Istvan Szepsy of Tokaji.

It was Noël Pinguet who was instrumental in turning the Huët domaine over to Biodynamism, one of the first important French estates to do so. "When I arrived I knew nothing — neither much about winemaking nor about Biodynamics," says Pinguet. "But I was disturbed by the chemicals and pesticides being used in the vineyards. I wanted to protect the environment, not destroy it. Then I began to hear of what Nicolas Joly was doing. I went down to Savennières to meet him. I was impressed."

"Did Gaston Huët resist this move?" I enquire. "There was no problem," says Pinguet. "He was already a convert to homeopathy. We did trials under the supervision of Jacques Puisais [the famous local *oenologue* and professor]. These began in 1988. From 1990 we have been completely Biodynamic."

But does it work? "Even if Biodynamics didn't produce better wine," replies Pinguet with a grin, "at least I'd have the satisfaction of knowing that I am not destroying the environment. But, in fact I have the impression that the Bio-wines are purer and more elegant. They express their terroirs more. And my objective is to produce the most natural wines possible, representative of the vintage and their origins."

What are the differences, the personalities of the three great Huët terroirs? "In Le Haut *lieu-dit* we have a three- or four-metre (ten- or thirteen-foot) deep layer of clay, mixed with

OPPOSITE *By following Biodynamic principles on all parts of the Huët estate, Noël Pinguet believes each vineyard expresses both its origin and the vintage more clearly*

ABOVE *Harvest time at the Huët estate*

a little limestone. This is a heavy soil. So the wines are supple, easy to drink, soft and early to mature. Le Mont lies on the first *coteaux*, nearest to the Loire. Here the soil is very stony. There is less clay, even a bit of sand. It has a greenish touch to it. The resultant wine is feminine and austere, mineral and very elegant. In the Clos du Bourg the surface soil is less deep, hardly one metre (3.3 feet), and so the vine roots quickly penetrate into the limestone rock underneath. Here we get fatter, more substantial wines which need to be kept. While the wines of Le Mont are often *sec*, those from Clos du Bourg are normally *demi-sec* or richer still."

It all depends on the vintage, of course. Those where the conditions were the least favourable, such as 1972, 1984, 1987, and 1994, will yield *sec* wines, or be made into sparkling. Average years such as 1992, 1993, 1998, 1999, and 2000 will give *moelleux* and *demi-sec* wines from the *première trie*, *sec* and *mousseux* from the second. In good years such as 1985, 1986, 1988, 1995, 1996, and 2001 they will make a bit of *sec*, but most will be *demi-sec* or *moelleux*. While in exceptional years such as 1947, 1959, 1989, 1990, and 1997 it could be almost entirely *moelleux*. Noël Pinguet dislikes the use of the word *doux*. He prefers to talk about *moelleux* — some 30 grams per litre of residual sugar, and *moelleux première trie*, where the sugar level is 60–100.

Charles Joguet

LOIRE

THE EXTENSIVE JOGUET DOMAINE PRODUCES SOME OF THE BEST
CHINONS, AND BY CHOOSING A WINNING TEAM TO CONTINUE HIS GOOD
WORK, CHARLES JOGUET HAS ENSURED A BRIGHT FUTURE FOR HIS WINERY.

Charles Joguet was born in May 1931 into a peasant family of mixed farmers. His father grew
cereals as well as vines, kept pigs, and went hunting for truffles in the local woods. Charles,
though, had other ambitions. He wanted to be an artist. As soon as he was old enough he
escaped to Paris. Good as he is at it, the production of wine has always been a second interest
to him. He is a man of great charisma, and until his recent retirement, happy to be the front
man at the domaine. But the major exercise of his talent was in his selection of the team who
are really responsible for the Clos de la Dioterie and the other wines.

In 1984 Michel Pinard was appointed head winemaker. The following year Jacques Genet,
an accountant, was brought into the business. Genet owned land west of Chinon in Beaumont-en-Véron. In 1988 thirteen hectares of this was planted on sandy-clay terroir, which today produces the Cuvée Terroir. Finally in 1986 Alain Delaunay, then owner of a wine shop in Chinon but trained as an optician, was brought in as *régisseur* and operations manager. It was at this time that Charles Joguet began to retire. Effectively the triumvirate of Genet (general manager), Pinard, and Delaunay has been responsible for the wines ever since. Today they are responsible for forty hectares.

LEFT *The Joguet cellars lie at the foot of the famed*
Clos de la Dioterie

Chinon, of course, is made from the Cabernet Franc grape, known locally as the Breton. While this is a variety which will ripen happily in Bordeaux, full maturity can be a problem in Chinon, more than 300 kilometres (186 miles) to the north. The first step at this domaine is to prune to five buds, spaced out along the cane to avoid any possibility of rot. "This will give us 40 hl/ha," says Delaunay. "We will eliminate the counter-buds and double flowers when necessary. And all this will avoid having to green harvest later on unless the crop looks like being very abundant. The older vineyards, like the 2.2-hectare Clos de la Dioterie, are ploughed. But where the vines are young the natural vegetation is left in order to restrain the vines' vigour.

"We are much more vigilant about picking through the fruit in the vineyard at harvest time in order to eliminate anything sub-standard than we used to be," Delaunay continues. "And also about the date we pick. The Cabernet Franc is not a variety for *sur*-maturity, but nevertheless we want to pick it as ripe as possible."

One of the chief red-winemaking challenges in the Loire is obtaining tannins which are ripe, and isolating those which are not. To this end, with the Dioterie and the other *vins de garde*, the fruit is entirely destemmed, cold-macerated for a day or two, fermented at 25–26°C (77–79°F), with *pigeage* as well as *remontage* (pumping over of juice), and macerated for fifteen to eighteen days, raising the temperature to 35°C (95°F) briefly at the end. The malolactic fermentation takes place in barrel. But the wood is old. Bottling is carried out about fourteen months after that. With the lesser *cuvées* the procedure is similar, but there is no *pigeage*, the length of the maceration is shorter, and the wines are not aged in barrel.

Joguet has a number of small barrel cellars at its winemaking headquarters in Sazilly, but some six kilometres (3.7 miles) away in Marcay, under the Clos de la Dioterie, a vast old quarry provides a most impressive environment. In its previous life, this cellar had always been used not for storing wine but for mushroom growing, so it is still very white. This magnificent space is used for receptions.

I like the Joguet wines. They are clean, fresh, and balanced, and even at the *vin de garde* end, essentially fruit-driven, which is not to say that top vintages of Dioterie or Chêne Vert do not need a decade for them to arrive at their optimum. Lesser wines such as the Cuvée Terroir, the Cuvée Les Petites Roches, and the Cuvée de la Cure, of course, mature sooner. They can be consumed slightly chilled, like Beaujolais.

The Clos de la Dioterie, however, is the Joguet domaine's best wine. In vintages like 1989 — and perhaps 2002, so early prognostications indicate — we have a great wine. The 1990, 1995, 1996, and 2001 are also remarkably good.

rhône

Differences in soils, grape varieties, and microclimates give southern Rhône, centred around Châteauneuf-du-Pape, a vastly different vinous portfolio to the north, chiefly Hermitage and Côte-Rôtie.

Beaucastel

RHONE

THE PERRIN FAMILY PARTNERS AN ECO-FRIENDLY APPROACH IN THE
VINEYARD WITH UNIQUE VINIFICATION METHODS TO MAKE BEAUCASTEL
WINES THE FINEST IN CHATEAUNEUF-DU-PAPE.

Château de Beaucastel, the leading estate in Châteauneuf-du-Pape, lies to the northeast of the area, on the edge of the motorway which runs round the side of the appellation. It has belonged to the Perrin family since 1921. Responsibility now lies with François Perrin, born in 1954. There are 100 hectares under vines, seventy within the Châteauneuf-du-Pape region, and thirty across the motorway making an excellent Côtes du Rhône called Cru du Coudoulet. The vineyards are planted as follows: ten per cent white grapes (Grenache Blanc, Clairette, Bourboulenc, Roussanne, Picpoul, and Picardin), ten per cent Vaccarèse, Muscardin, and Terret Noir, thirty per cent Grenache, thirty per cent Mourvèdre, ten per cent Syrah, and five each of Cinsault and Counoise: all thirteen authorized varieties. As you will notice, the Mourvèdre percentage is unusually high. This is deliberate. The Perrins swear by it. "If Beaucastel has a reputation," says François, "it is thanks to the Mourvèdre."

Beaucastel is perfectionist in its viticultural methods. Since 1964, no chemical pesticides, herbicides, or artificial fertilizer have been used in the vineyard. The land is manured with sheep dung and the previous year's skins, pips, and stalks, and the vines merely treated with *bouillie bordelaise* (copper sulphate solution) and sulphur against various forms of mildew.

The vinification methods at Beaucastel are unique to the property, and largely responsible for the individuality and quality of the wine. The grape bunches are entirely destemmed (this is now becoming more and more common elsewhere in the appellation). Then, without crushing, they are heated to 80°C (176°F) for around two minutes as they are pumped towards the vats, and then rapidly cooled back to normal temperatures.

This flash heating process — a form of pasteurization — affects only the skins of the grapes, and has been going on since the war, following experiments by the late Jacques Perrin and his father. The object is to aid the extraction of colour and fruit by softening the skins, and also to kill the polyphenoloxidase enzymes which cause wine to oxidize quickly. Because of this it is not necessary to sulphur the grapes and must as much as elsewhere. It is also, surprisingly, not necessary to add artificial yeasts. Though much of the yeast which is naturally present on

ABOVE *Plenty of stone galets,*
characteristic of the Châteauneuf-
du-Pape appellation, at the
entrance to Château de Beaucastel

ABOVE *Knocking the stakes into*
the rocky terrain prior to
replanting a vineyard at
Château de Beaucastel

the skin of the grape must be killed, there is enough left, in the opinion of the Perrins, in the cellar and in the vineyard to compensate.

Thereafter the berries are pumped into the fermentation vats and the *cuvaison* takes place for about fifteen days, controlled at 25—30°C (77—86°F). Subsequently the final juice is extracted by a Willmes press; the wine from the different grapes blended in February or March, and the wine matured in oak *foudres* (fifty-hectolitre capacity or smaller) for a further year and a couple of months before bottling. The wine is not filtered.

In 1989 the Perrins produced a special red wine *cuvée*, Hommage à Jacques Perrin, in honour of their father. François and his brother Jean-Pierre were tasting the various elements of this brilliant vintage, prior to the creation of the Beaucastel blend, when they came across a *foudre* of old-vine Mourvèdre that was so stupendous it cried out for special treatment. They isolated this, found some complementary wine, including some particularly good Counoise, and bottled it separately. The Hommage is simply the best young Châteauneuf I have ever sampled.

At any one time Beaucastel will have the equivalent of five vintages maturing in the cellar, a great deal more than most Châteauneuf-du-Pape estates. Because of space constraints, many properties cannot bottle an entire vintage in one go; and as a result bottles can vary enormously. To avoid this problem a new storage cellar was constructed at Beaucastel in 1981, three times as large as the older one, in order to be able to bottle the entire harvest at the optimum moment.

Beaucastel is one of the finest and longest-lasting Châteauneuf-du-Papes. About 2,200 hectolitres (nearly 25,000 cases) are produced annually, and it normally takes some six years to come into its own. As with most of the wines of the area, Beaucastel is full-bodied, sturdy and meaty, with a robust hardness — even fieriness — when immature, but a solid, warm richness pervades when it is ready for drinking. What distinguishes Beaucastel from the run of the mill is its inherent elegance — a word not often used for the wines of the area — albeit in a rather opulent, even aggressive, spicy, and aromatic manner. Quite simply, it is usually the best wine in the appellation. It also ages well in bottle.

Jean-Louis Chave

RHONE

WITH OVER 500 YEARS IN THE AREA, THE CHAVES HAVE AN INTIMATE KNOWLEDGE OF WHAT EACH OF THEIR VINEYARDS CAN GIVE TO THE FINAL BLEND, MAKING THEM THE MASTERS OF HERMITAGE.

The Chave family has been growing grapes on the Hermitage hill since 1481, an unbroken tradition that must be unrivalled anywhere else in the Rhône Valley, if not throughout the wine-growing countries of Europe.

The Chaves, alternate generations being christened Jean-Louis, the name of the domaine, live at Mauves, on the other side of the Rhône from Hermitage, a few kilometres south of Tournon. Not for them, however great the reputation of the wine, a grand country house, Porsche at the front door or swimming pool at the back. The Chave house is modest but comfortable, and lies directly on the main street of Mauves, with only a discreet, rather battered, rusty metal sign to let you know where they are, and to post you up a narrow side alley to the back entrance and access to the cellars. This is, of course, a family affair. Gérard Chave, *paterfamilias*, is today in his sixties; Jean-Louis, his son, is in his thirties. Responsibility for the wine is shared between them, while it is Monique, Gérard's wife, who runs the commercial side of the business.

The Chaves have five hectares of white grapes on the Hermitage hill and ten hectares of red. The white grapes — between eighty and ninety per cent Marsanne, and ten and twenty per cent Roussanne (they can't be more specific because some of the older vines are mixed plantings) — come from two types of soil at the eastern end of the 130-hectare appellation: limestone, which gives the wine richness and a Victoria plum flavour; and loess, which produces a balancing acidity, and gives white-flower aspects on the palate. "You can make good red in these white wine soils," says Jean-Louis, "but not vice versa. If the white varietals are not planted in the right soil the wine tends to be too alcoholic, too flat. We need a balancing glycerol in the wine to give it interest and grace."

There are at least three more very different soil structures for the red grapes, mainly Syrah of course. At the western end, in the *climat* of Bessards, for instance, the composition is based on granite. This will give you the structure. L'Hermite, a little more to the east, and higher up, is loess, and will give you the spiciness characteristic of Hermitage. Méal, lower down, is a limestone-based soil filled with quartz stones: this gives flesh and floral tones, while Peléat,

ABOVE *Bunches of grapes drying on straw mats. These will be vinified to make the rare, sweet vin de paille*

a brown sandy-pebbly mixture, imparts purity and aroma. The Chaves also have vines in the loamy *climats* of Greffieux and Diognières, lower down, which give finesse and scented fruit, and in the red marly soils of Beaumes and Rocules, half-way up, adding delicacy, elegance, and, in the best years, a voluptuous touch.

None of these, however, is complete on its own. The art of Hermitage is the art of the blend. The explanation why the Chave Hermitage is the best wine of the appellation is not only that they are rare in having vines in all these *climats*, but that they are geniuses in this art, the creation of something that is greater than the sum of its parts.

Today the grapes are 100 per cent destemmed. As the fermentation proceeds, the *chapeau* (cap of skins) is trodden down into the juice twice daily, thus helping to extract colour and tannin. The timing of the length of maceration, must with skins, is crucial. Too long a *cuvaison* and the resultant wine will become too tannic, too sturdy, too tough. Too little and it will lack structure and backbone. The point at which to decant (*écouler*) all depends on the quality of the original fruit. "Hermitage is not necessarily a big wine," says Jean-Louis. "What is more important is that the fruit is ripe and the elements are in balance. We're looking for finesse rather than power."

The resulting wine, of course, is splendid. It is rather more austere than the Jaboulet Hermitage La Chapelle, not nearly as oaky. The acidity seems higher, the fruit and flower flavours also more high-toned. Ten years is the barest minimum before the wine is ready for drinking. Twenty would be better still.

In 1990, for the first time, the Chaves released a Cuvée Cathelin. They don't always declare it, and it doesn't necessarily denote a superior vintage, for they produced a 1991, a good-but-not-brilliant vintage, and did not make a 1999, a splendid year. So far there have been four Cathelins: 1990, 1991, 1995, and 1998. Two thousand bottles are usually produced.

The Chaves are at pains to point out that this is not a super-*cuvée*, merely a different blend. There is no pre-ordained recipe. All the seven *lieux-dits* are used. "It depends on the vintage," says Jean-Louis. "Our endeavour is to get the balance right."

ABOVE *The Peléat vineyard in Hermitage. Fruit from here produces wine that imparts purity and aroma to the eventual Chave blend*

Guigal

RHONE

THROUGH PATIENCE AND PERSISTENCE, GUIGAL HAS BUILT UP FABULOUS
HOLDINGS IN THE NORTHERN RHONE, PRODUCING AN ARRAY OF WINES
THAT MORE THAN EARNS HIM THE TITLE, KING OF COTE-ROTIE.

In the heart of the Côte-Rôtie *vignoble* are the two famous *côtes*, the Brune and the Blonde.
There are perhaps no more than a dozen hectares under vine in each. The main *climats* in
the Côte Brune are La Viaillière, Côte Rosier, La Turque, La Pommière, La Chevalière, La Côte
Boudin, Le Pavillon Rouge, and La Landonne. Those of the Côte Blonde are La Chatillonne,
La Grande Plantée, Grand Clos, and La Mouline. Of these Maison Guigal has the monopoly
of three: La Mouline, La Landonne, and La Turque.

The total family holding in the Côte-Rôtie is fourteen hectares, acquired painstakingly, piece
by piece, over the years. The surface area of La Mouline is one lone hectare, while that in La
Landonne measures three hectares on the *cadastre* (the local land register) although at present
only two are under vine. This vineyard was formerly owned by seventeen separate growers.
"You can't imagine the trouble we had to go through to acquire it. It took us ten years, buying
each plot individually. But I have no doubt it will be worthwhile," Marcel Guigal said at the
outset. The Turque vineyard used to belong to a curious character called André Cachet. He
refused to comply with all the bureaucracy which went with the introduction of *appellation
contrôlée* in the 1930s and let his vines decay into weeds. The major wine company, Vidal-
Fleury, bought the land in 1974 and replanted it in 1980. Guigal later took the vineyard over,
with his first vintage being 1985.

Guigal's three top wines are named after these three *lieux-dits*. La Mouline was first
launched in 1966 and they currently make some 4,500–6,000 bottles a year. La Landonne
was introduced in 1978. Today some 10,000 bottles are produced. La Turque appeared with
the 1985 vintage, again in small quantities. The Guigals have more vineyards in the two *côtes*,
at Le Pavillon and La Pommière for instance, and from these they produce their Château
d'Ampuis. Additionally there is a Côte-Rôtie, Brune et Blonde, helped by the wine from
grapes brought in from other suppliers in the area.

All these wines are of exceptional quality. The Brune et Blonde is a very fine, new-oaky
Côte-Rôtie. Marcel Guigal will tell you that the flavour of Côte-Rôtie should combine
blackberry, mulberry, and a little raspberry. "Never blackcurrant. That is Hermitage."

ABOVE *The Château d'Ampuis on the Rhône with the steep vineyards of Côte-Rôtie in the background*

ABOVE *The charming Château d'Ampuis, home to Guigal, the unarguable "King of Côte Rôtie"*

La Mouline, grown in soil of limestone, mica, and flint debris in the Côte Blonde, and with the benefit of some eleven per cent Viognier in the blend (in volume; there is some thirteen per cent in terms of vines on the slope) is a wine of intense flavour, less structured than the Landonne, which evolves after eight to ten years in bottle into something of great complexity and delicacy (in Côte-Rôtie terms), with a freshness, an individuality, and a herbal element which comes from the addition of the Viognier. La Landonne, on the other hand, is purely Syrah, and comes from a soil with rather less limestone in its composition. This is an altogether different wine, one of substance, richness, and power, characterized by its raw Syrah fruit in its youth and not mellowing until it has attained at least ten years of age. La Turque is even more individual. Marcel Guigal describes it as a hermaphrodite, a Brune with Blonde characteristics. It has a flavour of black cherries, rare for a Côte-Rôtie. The first vintage, the 1985, was unbelievably good for a young-vine wine.

Guigal's Côte-Rôtie spends longer in wood than almost any other red wine in France — up to 3.5 years. Few others are as willing or as able to be so traditional in their approach. Moreover maturation or *élevage* is entirely in new oak. The casks are made in Burgundy from wood from the Tronçais forest in central France. A new-oak cask develops a wine's bouquet faster than the *foudre*, Guigal will tell you. He is not a believer in old wood. After a while the cleanliness cannot be guaranteed, he says, and there is a danger of the casks imparting undesirable taints to the wine. His wines are neither fined nor filtered.

Guigal's top Côte-Rôties are wonderful wines: rich and full-bodied and succulent, firm but not sturdy, and capable of lasting twenty years or more. Of the three, my favourite is La Landonne. It is the most classic. It has the most finesse.

Paul Jaboulet Aîné

RHONE

ONE OF THE WORLD'S MOST SUMPTUOUS, AGEABLE WINES, RETAINING A VIVACIOUS FRESHNESS EVEN IN MATURITY, HERMITAGE LA CHAPELLE IS THE BEST KNOWN AND ONE OF THE FINEST WINES OF THE APPELLATION.

Paul Jaboulet Aîné owns 29.5 out of the 130 hectares of vine on the hill of Hermitage, including the land on which lies the tiny, dilapidated chapel of St-Christophe near the top of the hill, and from which they take the fruit for their most famous wine. Twenty-five of these hectares are planted with the Syrah grape and those which traditionally produce La Chapelle lie in the *climats* of Le Méal (six hectares in total) and Les Bessards (nineteen hectares). The remaining 4.5 hectares grow the Marsanne and Roussanne varieties from which they make their celebrated white Hermitage, Le Chevalier de Stérimberg. The vines are replaced when they are sixty-five to seventy years old, thus maintaining an average age of thirty-five years or so.

Cultivation on the steep hill is a problem. Though spraying these days is done by helicopter, estate manager Philippe Jaboulet still reckons on one labourer per hectare on the hill rather than one per ten hectares on the flatter Crozes vineyards. The terrain is steep and the fragile layer of topsoil has to be protected within terraces, or too much would be washed away every time there was a thunderstorm. Machines are just beginning to be evolved which can work the soil efficiently, some of which have been invented by the Jaboulets themselves, but much of the ploughing is still done using horses and mules.

The harvest of the Syrah grape normally takes a fortnight and commences about two-thirds of the way through September, after the white wine varieties have been picked. Care has to be taken because the vines in the different *climats* mature at different intervals. Otherwise the whole 29.5 hectares could have been cleared in five days.

Since 1988 the grapes have been 100 per cent destemmed before being crushed. For two or three days the temperature is allowed to rise — as it will, naturally, for fermentation gives off heat — to 30°C (86°F), in order to extract the maximum amount of colour. Thereafter the vats are cooled to 26–28°C (79–82°F) and the *cuvaison*, during which the juice is in contact with the skins, continues for three or even four weeks.

The Jaboulets are very specific about the oak they use for maturing, not only La Chapelle, but all their red wines. They are wary of new oak. La Chapelle is matured in one-third new oak, from François Frères in Burgundy, and two-thirds older wood.

In most years all the Hermitage Jaboulet produce is sold as La Chapelle. Exceptionally, in weaker vintages such as 1992 and 1993, some of the lesser vats are rejected and appear as simple Hermitage.

Hermitage La Chapelle is one of the fullest, densest, and richest wines in the world. It is also one of the longest-lived. When young the colour is immense: a solid, viscous, almost black–purple that continues to the very rim of the glass. The nose is leafy, with an undercurrent of unripe blackcurrants, and though the new oak percentage is small, the effect is clearly discernible. The wine is full-bodied and very tannic; strong, powerful, and alcoholic, but not fiery; clean as a whistle, without anything robust or spicy about it despite the "size" of the wine.

Hermitage La Chapelle rarely matures before its tenth birthday. Twenty years is par for the course for the very best vintages, and they will keep for a further twenty or more thereafter. When mature, La Chapelle is not just an impressive glass of wine: it is nectar. The backbone, of course, remains, but the wine within the structure is rich, ample, profound, and aromatic, with a depth of flavour and a concentration of character that have few rivals. The fruit is now a ripe and subtle combination of blackcurrant and blackberry with a hint of raspberry, all underpinned by a slightly baked smell, as if the wine could remember its origins as the sun slowly heated up the granite day after day while the grapes were ripening. What I find breathtaking about La Chapelle is the extraordinary retention of fresh, ripe fruit, even in a wine that is over twenty years old.

This is one of the world's most exciting wine areas, full of young, dedicated, enthusiastic *vignerons* whose only aspiration is to produce the finest wine they can.

Gauby

ROUSSILLON

WITHIN TWO DECADES OF BOTTLING THEIR OWN WINE, AN AVERSION TO
OVERPRODUCTION PLUS A PASSIONATE AFFINITY WITH THE LOCAL SOILS
HAVE MADE DOMAINE GAUBY THE BEST ESTATE IN THE ROUSSILLON.

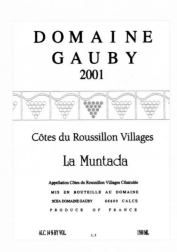

"A good consultant oenologist is a dead one," says the forty-four-year-old Gérard Gauby.
"All decisions about wine should be made as a result of tasting." Yes, you'll make mistakes
from time to time, but you will realize that they are mistakes quicker on the palate than
by analyzing the wine in the laboratory. Besides, "I want to make my wine; not someone
else's."

Some twelve years ago I was in the Midi. I wanted to sample the highly regarded 1989
and 1990 Roussillon vintages, by then in bottle. I asked the local wine-growers' association
to set up a blind tasting. This they duly did, informing me that the bottles would be lined
up *chez* Gauby, in Calce.

Calce turned out to be quite a long way from anywhere, deep into the limestone or
schistous *garrigue* at about the point where Côtes du Roussillon becomes Côtes du Roussillon
Villages. Nevertheless the village was easy to find, and the Gauby winery, at the entrance to
the village, impossible to miss. I found Gérard and his attractive wife Ghislaine to be
immediately *sympas*, and was consequently more than pleased, when we uncovered the bottles,
to discover that I had placed the Gauby Vieilles Vignes top of my list in both vintages. We
have been friends ever since.

I had arrived at the right time. Gérard's grandfather looked after five hectares, and sent the
result to the local cooperative until 1983. Gérard's first vintage was 1988. He immediately set
about enlarging the estate, buying plantation rights in the plain and transferring them to the
Calce hills which none of the locals were interested in developing.

Compared with the Languedoc, which includes, *inter alia*, Corbières, Minervois, St-Chinian,
and Faugères, the Roussillon, farther south towards the Spanish border, has been slow in
evolving into the modern age. There are two main reasons for this: the dominance of the
local cooperatives (once in the cooperative machine, for one is effectively a shareholder, it is
difficult as well as expensive to extract oneself) and the importance of the local sweet wines,
Banyuls, Maury, and the ubiquitously produced Muscat de Rivesaltes. The emergence of good,
individual domaines has been slow. There are still only a few dozen, compared with the

ABOVE *Gauby vines in the*
schistous soil above Calce, where
Côtes du Roussillon meets Côtes
du Roussillon Villages

hundreds farther north. Yet, geologically and climatically, up in the hills, this is an ideal spot to produce interesting wine.

"One of our great advantages is the complexity of our local soils," he says. "We have schist of various colours, schist with clay, limestone of various types, from pure rock to marl, and even *grès* (a purple-coloured hard sandstone rock). Schist is the best as you get deep, complex root systems which give vines that never suffer from drought even in the driest of summers. And wines with very good acidities. At first I planted lots of Syrah, to add to those planted in the 1980s; later Mourvèdre, some of it ungrafted. We took up Biodynamism in 1996. From 2001 the domaine has been completely Biodynamic."

The Gaubys have two grown-up children, Lionel and Mélanie, and it was the twenty-year-old Lionel who made the 2002 and 2003. They prune and de-bud with an objective of producing an average of 35 hl/ha. "I feel I've failed if I have to green harvest," says Gérard. The small harvest means there is no blocking of the maturity of the phenolic elements.

In 2003 they moved from the entrance to Calce to a new winery and dwelling house five kilometres (three miles) outside the village, along a deliberately unmarked winding lane, right in the middle of the vineyards. It is a small corner of paradise.

Since 1995 the Gaubys have been concentrating on two red wines. As well as the Grenache-Carignan-Syrah/Mourvèdre Vieilles Vignes (usually fifty : thirty : twenty in percentage terms), a wine called Muntada from the *lieu-dit* around the new winery was launched. At first this was 100 per cent Syrah and almost 100 per cent new oak. Today it is a sort of super-selection of the *vieilles vignes*, containing between forty and fifty-five per cent Syrah, and the amount of new oak has also been reduced.

These wines are made after three to five days of cold-soaking, sometimes with a small percentage of the stems, sometimes with a couple of *pigeages*. The *cuvaison* can range from five days to a month. The wines are blended after six months. The Vieilles Vignes is bottled after the second winter, sixteen to eighteen months on, the Muntada after twenty to twenty-six months.

"I don't like *sur-maturité*," explains Gérard. "I'm looking for fresh fruit. Burgundy is my reference. I want the same purity in my wines."

The Côtes du Roussillon Vieilles Vignes is an impressive wine: complex, minerally, balanced, and pure. With fine acidity and very good tannins it is a Midi wine of real class. In the best of vintages, like a good claret, it needs ten years. The Muntada has changed. The 1998 is an overweight, over-oaked brute of a wine. It failed to live up to its early promise. But now the wine, while unmistakably Syrah-based, is much richer and more complex. It is a full, rich wine of great finesse. It's not cheap. But it's worth it.

La Grange des Pères

LANGUEDOC

LA GRANGE DES PERES IS FOR ME THE GREATEST DOMAINE IN
THE LANGUEDOC. THOUGH RECENT, THE WINES ARE ALREADY
THE MOST PROFOUND AND SOPHISTICATED OF THE REGION.

Wild boars love grapes. Back in 1995 Laurent Vaillé's first harvest of white wine was largely consumed by the beasts before the family could get out and collect the fruit. To avoid *sanglier* depredation, says Laurent, what you need to do is to catch and butcher one, and expose bits of the flesh at strategic points in the vineyard. The smell puts off the remainder of the group.

The Vaillé family has been established in Aniane for centuries. As well as cereals they had vines, which in recent generations were turned into wine by the local cooperative. Laurent's father, however, gave up being a *vigneron*. It was uneconomic. Cereals were less work, and more profitable. He told his children Bernard, now forty-four, and Laurent, forty-one, not to think of living off the land. Go and get a professional qualification, he said. So Laurent took his advice and trained as an osteopath.

The Vaillé family likes to live well. And food and wine are important elements in their art of good living. So the lure was there. Laurent decided that, after all, he had to become a *vigneron*. Low-quality wine was obviously not an option. But others in the Midi had already shown that making wine at the quality end could be viable. Domaine de Trévallon was an example of what could be achieved from scratch.

The first priority was to find the right sites. The land round Aniane is undulating and mostly limestone, watered by underground springs. Much of the potentially best vineyard land was lying fallow, *en friche*, given up since the phylloxera epidemic because it was too hard and stony to work, or because it was on north-facing cooler slopes. This was exactly what Laurent was looking for. Parcels where the sugars would not be ready until the tannins were fully ripe. "In order to make a good wine you have absolutely got to have a stony soil," he says. One of his vineyards, northwest of Aniane, resembles Châteauneuf-du-Pape. Another, high up on the road to La Boissière, is broken-up limestone rock, as at Trévallon, and exposed to the east and north. "We are 300 metres above sea level here," he adds. "Sometimes you can see the Pyrénées. But if so it will rain tomorrow."

In 1989 Laurent Vaillé planted his first vines. While waiting for them to grow he enrolled at Montpellier to study oenology, and worked for Eloi Dürrbach at Trévallon. Subsequently he

went to learn from Chave and Jean-François Coche in Meursault. "Like a composer, you study the great masters," he is quoted as saying. "But that doesn't mean you should copy them."

Laurent's first red wine vintage was 1992, the white dating from 1995. The latter is now made from ninety-plus per cent Roussanne with a dash of Chardonnay and Marsanne. It is vinified entirely in new oak and bottled after two years. The red comes from Syrah, Mourvèdre (cuttings from Château de Beaucastel), and Cabernet Sauvignon (forty : forty : twenty) with one barrel's-worth of 100-year-old Carignan. Yields are low — usually around 18–25 hl/ha — thirty per cent new wood is employed, and bottling takes place after two years, the blend being made at the last minute. The reason that both colours are bottled so late is that the *cave*, which is underground, is very cold. The malolactic fermentations take a long time to finish, and the wine evolves very slowly.

Vaillé is against what he terms "modern fads": micro-oxygenation, malolactic in barrel, *delastage*, etc. The red wine is vinified, after total destemming, in stainless steel with *pigeage* but no *remontage*, and the maceration times vary from year to year and grape variety to grape variety.

The wine was an almost instant success, thanks largely to the support of those where Laurent had done his *stages* and other friends.

So, what has changed since 1992? "As life goes on," says Laurent, "and we mature as well as our wines, I begin to understand each parcel better [the domaine now covers fourteen hectares]. I know which mature sooner, which later. And I vinify with the final assembled wine in mind. I can nuance each *cuvée* better now."

"At the beginning I didn't have the means to purchase the necessary to do the *élevage* properly. And I also over-extracted. I've cut the *pigeages* down to one rather than two. Also at the beginning our suppliers did not know the estate. We now get first pick of the best barrels, corks, etc. We are more perfectionist now."

La Grange des Pères, if it can be compared with anything, has a resemblance to Trévallon, but with less of a *garrigue*, wild-herb touch, and with higher-toned fruit. Like Trévallon it is a wine built to last, needing at least a decade in most vintages, and with the exception of 2002, all the most recent vintages have been very good. Today, as evidenced by the 2001 and 2000, we have a wine that already has plenty of sophistication. Laurent Vaillé has obviously learned much from his mentors. The crisp, Hermitage-like white wine is very good too.

Montus

ALAIN BRUMONT FIRST GAINED RECOGNITION FOR HIS TANNAT WINES JUST TWENTY YEARS AGO, SINCE THEN HE HAS SINGLEHANDEDLY BROUGHT ABOUT THE RENAISSANCE OF THIS UNFASHIONABLE GRAPE.

Down in deepest southwest France, where the *départements* of Pyrénées-Atlantiques and Hautes-Pyrénées meet that of Gers, and where Gascon flair and Béarnais attrition combine to provide the nucleus of the French rugby football team, you will find the "old country", or the *vic-bilh* (*vic-bilh* means old country in the *langue d'oc*) and the wine of Madiran.

Forty years ago this was a dead area. Just as in Cahors, phylloxera and depression had dealt an almost deadly blow. Despite the granting of *appellation contrôlée* in 1948, there were barely a few dozen hectares under vine, and what they produced was rustic and unmemorable. Madiran in those days was tart and inky when it was young, astringent and dried out when it was mature, having been matured in *foudres* for several years. There was no new oak, no controlled fermentation, and the local grape, the somewhat muscular Tannat, was falling out of favour and in danger of being obscured under easier varieties such as Cabernet and Merlot.

Today, all has changed. The *vignoble* now covers 1,400 hectares. Tannat is properly recognized as a serious *vin de garde*-producing *cépage*. And there is a thriving band of domaine-bottling estates, many of whom produce top wines, *têtes de cuvées*. These days, the wines are increasingly worth noticing.

The greatest impetus behind Madiran's renaissance came from Alain Brumont. Brumont produced a *cuvée prestige* from five-year-old 100 per cent Tannat vines and 100 per cent new oak in 1985. At first the locals declined to give it the "label" of *appellation contrôlée*. The wine was then referred to a higher authority in Bordeaux. Back it came, both with AC status and a message. The message pronounced: "It is the best Madiran we've ever tasted." The press soon buzzed down to Madiran. Brumont's Montus was written up widely. "Best wine of the year," said some. Not to be outdone, one of France's influential wine and gastronomy magazines, *Gault Millau*, pronounced it "Wine of the Decade".

Alain Brumont was born in 1946. His father grew maize and made undistinguished wine (forty per cent Merlot in the blend, and as large a yield as nature would allow) at Château Bouscassé. Alain visited Bordeaux in 1979, and it was this experience which was to change his life. He returned determined to produce high-quality, largely Tannat wine. Singlehandedly he

ABOVE *The Brumont*
headquarters at
Château Bouscassé

took over and replanted the derelict Château Montus. It was the 1985 vintage of this wine which put Brumont — and Madiran — on the map.

Since 1985 Brumont has continued to expand — to the extent where he got into deep financial trouble in recent years (happily this now seems to have been resolved). He now controls over 200 hectares, plus a sizeable holding of *vin de pays*-producing land (Les Menhirs: Tannat and Merlot). Sixty per cent of this is fermented at Château Montus, forty per cent at Bouscassé.

The land is curious. Most of it is a clay–limestone mixture. You'll only get so-so wines from this soil. Most of it is planted with maize. Here and there, however, you will come across parcels impregnated with pudding stones, the *galets* you find at Châteauneuf-du-Pape. Here you will get good wine.

Château Bouscassé comes in two versions. The lesser wine is made from sixty-five per cent Tannat, twenty-five Cabernet Sauvignon, and ten Cabernet Franc, and is aged in older wood. The Vieilles Vignes — the vines are over fifty years old — comes exclusively from Tannat, which is macerated for a month and aged in 100 per cent new wood. This is a very serious wine indeed. A rival to the Montus Prestige.

The basic Montus comes from eighty per cent Tannat, fifteen per cent Cabernet Sauvignon, and five per cent Fer Servadou and is aged in fifty per cent new oak. This is a step above the lesser Bouscassé. The Cuvée Prestige is again pure Tannat, the product of a month-long *cuvaison* and 100 per cent new oak: minimal racking, no fining, no filtration.

La Tyre — the first vintage was 2000 — is from a splendidly sited fifteen-hectare vineyard: pure Tannat. Very impressive.

Tempier

PROVENCE

I HAVE LOVED THE WINES OF BANDOL'S DOMAINE TEMPIER SINCE I FIRST VISITED THE ESTATE AS A STUDENT IN 1964. THE COMBINATION OF THE 1952 AND THE PEYRAUD HOSPITALITY WAS INTOXICATING.

The Mourvèdre is the last undiscovered great red wine grape. When young, the wine it produces is full-bodied, unyielding, and somewhat bitter: brutal even. Not for the faint-hearted. With age — and it needs a decade or more — it will eventually mellow to give a wine with richness, warmth, and concentration, and a spicy complexity; and moreover, a wine with a surprising elegance. It is a variety that thrives in conditions which are hot and arid, and in the calcareous and siliceous schists of the south of France.

Only in one small area, however, is it actively promoted to the extent of being required to be the dominant quotient of the blend: in Bandol. Bandol is where you will find the expression of the Mourvèdre at its most untrammelled and — if you are patient enough — most triumphant. And in Bandol the best source is the Domaine Tempier at Le Plan du Castellet.

In the 1950s — there was only one red wine *cuvée* until 1968 — fifty per cent of Domaine Tempier was Mourvèdre. In 2001, even the basic wine had seventy per cent. The better *cuvées*: Spéciale from 1968, Migoua and Tourtine from 1979, Cabassaou from 1987, can have as much as ninety per cent of Mourvèdre in the blend. At first the majority of what they produced was *rosé*. Only since 1970 has more than half the wine been red.

Lucien Peyraud, who died in 1998, made over fifty vintages of Tempier. Progressively from 1974 onwards, he began to take a back seat, leaving his eldest son Jean-Marie to assume responsibility in the cellar, and his second son, François, to supervise the vineyards. The land is worked organically, as is increasingly common in the south of France.

You might expect the appellation of Bandol, bathed by the *provençal* heat, to provide uniform quality year after year. This is not the case. Even in the heat of the Midi, the Mourvèdre grape needs time to mature, and full maturation is paradoxically often retarded by drought. The harvest can begin as early as the first week of September, but can often prolong into October; particularly where, as may be the case elsewhere with some of the minor properties, the yield is not cut back, and the sun has to ripen an excessive amount of fruit. At Tempier, the Peyrauds take great pains to restrict the yield to 35 hl/ha. The last fifty years have seen a

regular succession of great vintages, and an increasing number of great Bandols as the individual *cuvées* have been isolated. I remember 1952, 1959, 1964, 1966, and the 1969, 1970, 1971 trio from my wine-merchant days. I have cellared the wine ever since I first visited Tempier. Since then we have had 1979, truly great wines in 1982 and 1990, and also in 1993. There has been another splendid trio in 1999, 2000, and 2001.

The wines are also uniform. There is as much variety as in Bordeaux or Burgundy. I remember a conversation I had with Lucien Peyraud in 1989. The 1970, he said, had a finesse which was very Bordelais. Lucien's musical analogy was Mozart. The 1971 was more a wine of the Midi, in my view. But Peyraud said it was Bach. The 1967, a wine of grace, charm, and femininity, he likened to Vivaldi. Would the 1975, a brooding, gamey, leathery giant of a wine be a Wagner then?

There is a marked difference between the single-vineyard wines. Migoua is the most elegant, a Palmer of a Bandol. It comes forward sooner than the Tourtine and the Cabassaou. These are more structured, more tannic, and often richer. But my vote usually goes to the Migoua.

Once in the Tempier winery the grapes are entirely destalked. There is sufficient tannin in the Mourvèdre skins already, and the stems, however brown and dry they may seem to the casual eye, are green inside. The varieties are blended together in stainless-steel fermentation vats, vinified at 25°C (77°F) or so, macerated with the skins for ten days and then racked off into large wooden *foudres* to complete their malolactic fermentation. The wine remains in wood for a minimum of eighteen months before bottling.

Jean-Marie and François Tempier are now in (or near) their sixties. There being no member of the family in the next generation willing to take over, the brothers took on the youthful and talented Daniel Ravier as manager in the late summer of 2000. Ravier has a decade's worth of experience in charge of other top estates in the appellation, notably at the Domaine de Souviou and at the Ott estates. A wise choice, I think.

LEFT *Domaine Tempier: those privileged to be invited to lunch dine under the trees on the left*
RIGHT *A young vineyard in the schistous soil of Bandol*

Trévallon

PROVENCE

TREVALLON IS NOT JUST THE GREATEST WINE OF PROVENCE BUT THE FINEST EXAMPLE OF A SYRAH/CABERNET SAUVIGNON BLEND. THE WINES ARE GETTING MORE AND MORE NOBLE AS THE VINEYARD AGES.

The first thing you notice here are the stones. And it comes as something of a shock. You have probably approached from Tarascon, to the west. Or St-Rémy, south of Avignon, and a dozen or so kilometres to the northeast. Indeed there is no other way to arrive. You have been bowling along plane-tree-lined roads bordered by lush fields of sweetcorn, greenhouses of cucumbers and peppers, and orchards of peaches and apricots. All interspersed with straight lines of cypress and other trees to protect the produce from the prevailing Mistral. This is mannered, managed Provence at its most archetypal: the fruit-basket of France.

Off one of these minor roads a gateway leads to a simple, but quite substantial, *provençal manoir* and the outbuildings of what could be any farming habitation in the south of France. Not a *maison de vacance*: it is too lived-in for that. And the rose garden and *potager* give evidence of year-in, year-out occupation. But nothing out of the ordinary. It is only when you leave the kitchen garden and the standard roses, cross a ditch, climb up a few metres away from the house that you enter a totally different landscape. On the north side civilization, on the other a wild moonscape of broken rock.

You are on the edge of Les Alpilles. It is here, literally dynamited out of the solid, craggy limestone rock, that Eloi Dürrbach, from 1974 onwards, blasted the surrounding *garrigues* into submission and planted a vineyard. It is here that one of the great and most individual wines of the Midi is produced. The birthplace of Trévallon is a savage and forbiddingly uncompromising rubble of rock, an abode of stones in which nature, grudgingly but triumphantly, allows a singular man to produce a singular wine. No other *provençal* wine is anything like it.

Today there are twenty hectares, in twenty different plots spread over several kilometres where the surrounding terrain was at its flattest and easiest to tame. One of these hectares is of white grapes: forty-five per cent Roussanne, forty-five per cent Marsanne, and ten per cent young Chardonnay. The remainder is sixty per cent Cabernet Sauvignon, forty per cent Syrah.

The development of Trévallon has been a learning curve in the civilizing of the tannins. The first few vintages were decidedly uncompromising: rugged, brutal, an untamed mixture

ABOVE *The Domaine de*
Trévallon, looking north.
In the foreground is the
moonscape of broken rock

of leather and tobacco and black fruit; the muscle and sinew hiding the fat and the flesh. Then came the 1982. Here was the first great wine, a justification at last for a decade of hope, ten years of brutalizing effort.

The next phase came with the 1988 and 1989. These make interesting foils to one another. In the earlier vintage it is the Cabernet which is to the fore. In the 1989 the Syrah dominates. The earlier vintage is cool and stylish. The later one is fat and lush, absolutely crammed with black fruit. The parallel with the Burgundy vintages is exact.

And, as in Burgundy, the apogee is the 1990. It has the fruit of the 1989, the balance of the 1988, and about twice the concentration of both put together. It is an utterly fabulous wine.

"Every time I serve the 1989 after the 1990", says Eloi, "it's destroyed. Now I serve the 1989 first." In the 1990, in fact, despite the percentages of varietals in the vineyard — which usually result in Cabernet : Syrah proportions of fifty-five : forty-five in the wine — there was more Syrah than Cabernet Sauvignon.

ABOVE *Young wine maturing in*
foudres in the Trévallon cellar

LEFT *The Trévallon domaine*
consists of a dozen or more tiny
vineyards hacked out of the
limestone rock

Progress has continued since, the wines getting increasingly more sophisticated and complex without losing any of their essential thrust or vigour. The 1994 is surprisingly good and the 1995 and 1998 both potentially excellent. I like the style of the 1999.

Harvests at Trévallon are low. In 1989, for instance, a mere 24 hl/ha. The largest there has ever been was in 1992 when Dürrbach made 34 hl/ha, and this is obviously a major factor in the enormous concentration of the wine, and its consistency even in so-called "poor" vintages. In fact there is no such thing as a bad Trévallon. The 1991 is certainly "good" at the very least, and the 1992 is even better, if not up to the potential glory of the 1990.

How do you describe the wine? Splendidly coloured. Impressively concentrated. Structured without being brutally solid. Balanced and complex. Those are the bare bones. And the flavours? Blackberry and blackcurrant, cedary and almost sweet in its richness, with an aspect of roasted wild Provencal herbs. It is a wine of the *garrigues*; it is a wine of uncompromising personality; and, like its origins, it is a wine of no half measures.

There is danger here. There is excitement. There is passion.

BORDEAUX

Ausone

Alain Vauthier
estate manager

Château Ausone
33330 St-Emilion
Tel: +33 5 57 24 24 57
Fax: +33 5 57 24 24 58
Email: chateau.ausone@
wanadoo.fr
red: Cabernet Franc, Merlot

The following vintages of Château Ausone were sampled in London at a tasting organized by the Institute of Masters of Wine and presided over by Alain Vauthier in January 2005.

RED WINE

CHATEAU AUSONE

Vintage 2002
Fine colour. Full, rich, cool nose. Very well-integrated oak. Fullish body. Very good tannins. Lovely ripe, elegant fruit. Very well balanced. This has a lovely long, lingering follow-through. Profound and multi-dimensional. Very fine.
2008–35

Vintage 2001
Good colour. Not as rich or as concentrated as the 2002 but very harmonious, fragrant, and elegant on the nose. Medium-full body. A little tannin. Essentially soft and potentially silky. Balanced and intense. Long and very fine for the vintage.
2010–25

Vintage 2000
Very good colour. Full, rich nose. Slightly robust and adolescent aspects at present. Fullish body. Rich and ample. Very ripe. At present a little all over the place. But there is good grip and very lovely fruit. The finish is impressive. Potentially the best of these first three wines.
2011–35

Vintage 1999
Very good colour. Slightly tight on the nose. Good fruit underneath but not up to the 2000/'01/'02 trio. Medium to medium-full body. Good fruit. Very good oak integration. Good grip. Long and multi-dimensional. Fine for the vintage.
2007–20

Vintage 1998
Very good colour. Quite a lot fatter and more substantial on the nose than the 1999. Full-bodied, rich and tannic. Cool and balanced. Lovely fragrant, flowery character. Very long. Very fine indeed for the vintage. The wine of the vintage?
2008–28

Vintage 1995
Medium-full colour. Some development. Slightly over-evolved on the nose. These bottles were not as they should be. Rather dry and fruitless. Medium body. The tannins are now round and mellow. Decent finish, some class but a lack of zip.
2005–12

Vintage 1989
Magnum. Medium-full, fully mature colour. Fragrant, developed but slightly rustic and roasted nose. Quite plump, but not very elegant. Nor very concentrated. Fully ready. Medium to medium-full body. Not a lot of structure. Decent acidity, but it lacks vigour and creaminess. Very good at best.
2005–12

Vintage 1985
Medium to medium-full, fully mature colour. A little dry on the nose but quite rich underneath. It lacks zip. Medium body. Ripe, soft, elegant, and fragrant. This is fresher than both the 1982 and the 1989. And I much prefer it. The wine is fully ready, mellow, yet long and positive and still with zip at the end. Fine.
2005–12+

Vintage 1982
Fullish, mature colour. Rich nose but a little astringent. Got drier as it developed. A second bottle was much fresher, richer, fatter, and more vigorous. Medium–full-bodied, ample, lush, exotic, and delicious. Fine (but only "good" for the first bottle: drink soon).
2005–12

Vintage 1978
Good vigorous, mature colour. Ripe but slightly austere on the nose. Medium-full body. Fresh. Stylish and fragrant. Now mellow. This is a lovely wine. Individual and flowery, but both generous and with good zip. Fine.
2005–10

key to notes: *years in italics indicate the timescales over which the author feels the wines are best to drink*

Cheval–Blanc

Pierre Lurton
estate manager

Château Cheval-Blanc
33330 St-Emilion
Tel: +33 5 57 55 55 55
Fax: +33 5 57 55 55 50
Email: contact@chateau-
chevalblanc.com
www.chateau-chevalblanc.com
red: Cabernet Franc, Merlot,
Cabernet Sauvignon

The following vintages of Château Cheval-Blanc, which came direct from the château, were offered at one of my Master tastings in November 2001.

RED WINE

CHATEAU CHEVAL-BLANC

Vintage 1998
Full colour. Opulent, rich, mocha, roast-chestnutty nose. Very impressive. Splendid depth here. Full, fat, and expansive. Very good tannin. Excellent grip. This is very classy. Marvellous ripe, multi-dimensional fruit. Very, very long. Very, very lovely. Excellent. The wine of the vintage.
2010–35

Vintage 1996
Medium-full colour. Good full nose. Rich and aromatic if without the power and intensity of the 1998. Firmer than the 1995. Medium-full body on the palate. A little tannin sticking out. Good fresh acidity. No lack of balance or elegance. Fine plus.
2006–20

Vintage 1995
Fullish colour. A little more profound than the 1996. Softer, riper, more opulent, more Merlot nose than the 1996. Medium-full body. Nice and fat and succulent. Better tannins than the 1996 and great definition and intensity. This has more to it than the 1996. Great depth and complexity. Very long. Very harmonious. Very fine plus.
2006–25

Vintage 1990
Fine colour. Barely mature. Rich nose. Not unlike the 1998 but obviously more developed. Plenty of structure. Plenty of depth. Still a little adolescent. Fullish body. A little unresolved tannin. Lots of depth. Very good juicy fruit and very good acidity. The 1998 is classier but this is very fine indeed. Lovely long finish.
2005–34

Vintage 1989
Very good colour. Plenty of vigour still. Soft, fresh, very aromatic nose. Sweet with a touch of both fondant and peppermint. Medium-full body. Smooth and less tannic but with less grip than the 1990. Now à *point*. The Merlot shows. Succulent and juicy. Most seductive. But not as serious as the 1990. Very fine though.
2005–18

Vintage 1988
Medium-full colour. Still youthful. Fresh nose. Plump and attractive. Not enormously structured but balanced and classy. Medium body. Fully ready. No hard edges. Ample, fresh, attractive, and harmonious. Very good positive finish. Almost as good as the 1989. Fine plus.
2005–18

Vintage 1985
Fullish, mature colour. Classy, cool, fresh, fragrant nose. Fuller and richer than the 1988 but not as opulent, as Merlot-y as the 1989. Fullish, very well balanced, understated, subtle but splendidly balanced wine. Very seductive at the end. Long and complex and delicious now. Not as big as the 1989 but a lot classier. Very fine plus.
2005–15

Vintage 1982
Full, mature colour. Opulent, fat, full, rich, quite Merlot nose. Full, succulent, seductive, and most attractive. But has it the greatest class? Or depth? Not this bottle. Sweet, ripe, rich, and with plenty of length. But I confess myself marginally disappointed. Very fine but not great. It lacks a bit of energy.
2005–15

Vintage 1975
Re-corked in 1999. Full, very fresh colour. Quite firm nose. Good spice. Just a little tannin. Fullish body. Some structure. Good grip. This is lush, fresh, and balanced, and rather better on the palate than on the nose. Good vigour. Nicely juicy, intense finish. Even better with food. An excellent example of the vintage.
2005–10

Haut-Brion

Jean-Bernard Delmas
former director

Château Haut-Brion
33608 Pessac
Tel: +33 5 56 00 29 30
Fax: +33 5 56 98 75 14
Email: info@haut-brion.com
www.haut-brion.com
red: Cabernet Sauvignon,
Merlot, Cabernet Franc

The following vintages of Château Haut-Brion were sampled in New London, New Hampshire, USA, at the end of September 2001. My thanks to my good friends Jack and Thelma Hewitt.

RED WINE

CHATEAU HAUT-BRION

Vintage 1996

Fullish colour but less pronounced than the 1995. Ripe and rich and still a bit raw and immature on the nose. Not an enormous amount of depth. Medium-full body. Still some tannin. Good balance and depth and there certainly is class. Classic but austere and backward. A slight lack of intensity and flair compared with the 1995. Fine though.
2005–26

Vintage 1995

Bigger colour than the 1996. Riper, fatter, and more aromatic on the nose. Fullish body. Good tannins. Very good concentration. This is richer and a lot more exciting than the 1996. Riper tannins. Good fat. Interesting depth, spice, and dimension. Very lovely, complex, classy finish. This is very fine.
2007–30

Vintage 1990

Fine colour but not the depth of the 1989. Rich, aromatic, very lovely nose. Full and tannic but the tannins are very well covered. Rich and succulent. Much more to it than the 1996 and 1995. This is very fine on the palate. Rich, complex, concentrated, and intense. Far superior to 1995 and 1996 if not as good as the 1989 (not quite!). Full body. Excellent tannins and grip. Long and very satisfying. Excellent. Lovely finish. Multi-dimensional.
2005–34

Vintage 1989

Splendidly concentrated colour. Marvellously ripe, succulent, rich nose. Great composure and intensity. Sweeter and more alcoholic than the 1990. Exotically fabulous. This has never been less than a very great wine. Very full. Excellent tannins. Enormous power and intensity and concentration of fruit. Something exotic. A Scheherazade of a wine. More or less perfect. Marvellous finish. It needs time.
2005–40

Vintage 1988

Very good colour. Similar to the 1990. No more sign of age. Most attractive nose. Very cool and classy and composed. Not the weight of 1989 and 1990 but very lovely. Real finesse. Marvellous balance. Medium-full body. A little tannin still. Very clear-cut. Not an enormous amount of intensity and dimension but what there is, is very composed. Very classy and long on the palate. Nearly there. Lots of juicy fruit. Most attractive and really elegant. Fine plus.
2005–20

Vintage 1986

Fine colour. Only a suspicion of maturity. Fuller and fatter than the 1988 but not as classy. Slightly burly in fact. This may well be a disappointing bottle. It seems evolved but astringent. A lack of grip. Perhaps bad storage. Medium-full body. Not enough composure and flair.
2005–12

Vintage 1985

Fuller, richer, fatter colour than the 1986. Still vigorous. Aromatic, classy nose. Lots of depth here. Much less diffuse than the 1986. Much more interest. It seems fully developed. Full body. Rich and beautifully balanced. Clearly the best between 1982 and 1989. Lovely vigorous fruit. Long and complex. Very fine indeed. Delicious.
2005–25+

Vintage 1983

Fullish colour. Rather more development than the 1985. Rich, but slightly burnt at the end on the nose. Getting diffuse now. The 1985 is fatter and has better grip, this 1983 is evolving fast. It has lost its class. Only medium body now. Some astringency. Decent fruit though and reasonably classy on the finish, but no depth.
2005–09

Vintage 1982

Full colour. Rather bigger than the 1983. More vigour too. Full, firm, fat, rich, and concentrated. Excellent grip. Lots of wine here. Lots of substance. But fine balance and very good depth. Still very vigorous, young and tannic. Even still a little dumb at first. Slightly four-square and slightly austere, yet lots of quality. As it evolved, obviously richer and more profound than the 1985. More intense too. Impressive. Very fine.
2005–20

Lafite-Rothschild

Charles Chevalier
estate manager

Château Lafite-Rothschild
33250 Pauillac
Tel: +33 5 56 73 18 18
Fax +33 5 56 59 26 83
www.lafite.com
red: Cabernet Sauvignon,
Merlot, Cabernet Franc,
Petit Verdot

These wines were offered at an Institute of Masters of Wine First Growth tasting seminar, presented by Charles Chevalier, in January 2003.

RED WINE

CHATEAU LAFITE-ROTHSCHILD

Vintage 1999
Good colour. Classy nose if not very rich or abundant. Cedary. Medium-full body. Quite soft tannins already. Decent grip but not an enormous backbone. Stylish but not a lot of concentration. Fine but not splendid, even in a 1999 context.
2008–20

Vintage 1998
Very good colour. Quite a bit richer and fuller than the 1999. Firm, oaky, ripe, and very classy. Fullish body. Good tannins. Still a bit unformed but very good grip. Lots of depth and dimension. This is long and complex and very elegant. Very fine indeed. In its context rather better than the 1999.
2011–30

Vintage 1996
Full colour. Still very youthful. Fullish, rich, concentrated nose. Lots of depth and class here. Slightly adolescent on the palate at present. Firm and slightly unyielding. Fullish body. Good tannins. Underneath, very lovely fruit well balanced by the acidity. More to it than the 1998 if less charm at present. Splendid fruit at the end. Very fine indeed for the vintage.
2011–30+

Vintage 1995
Medium-full colour. Just a little development. Good abundant nose. But not as much dimension or class as the 1996. Medium-full body. Soft and spicy. Neither the backbone nor the tannic structure of the 1996. Ripe and charming. Long and seductive. But the 1996 has more elegance, more depth. Very fine for the vintage.
2008–25

Vintage 1990
Fullish colour. Now some maturity. Lovely abundant nose. Cedary, harmonious, complex, and profound. Much classier than the 1989. Fullish body. Rich. The tannins just about absorbed. Very good grip. This is an exciting example. Very lovely fruit. Very well balanced. Lots of vigour. Very long. Excellent. Just about ready.
2005–30

Vintage 1989
Fullish, mature colour. Aromatic nose with slightly burly tannins. Ripe and full. Medium-full body. Soft, plump, fat, and succulent. Very good acidity. Much better on the palate than the nose. Really quite fresh. It doesn't have the class and backbone of the 1990 but a most attractive wine. Very fine indeed.
2005–15

Vintage 1988
If anything slightly more colour – and certainly less developed – than the 1989. Very stylish nose. Lovely fruit. Slight austerity, even a little hardness at first, but very complex and very elegant underneath. Medium-full body. The tannins are now just about rounded off but there is still a lot of vigour here. Ripe and balanced. Very good grip. Long. Very classy. Very lovely. Very fine indeed for the vintage.
2005–15

Vintage 1986
Full, mature colour. Still quite tight on the nose at first. Full and firm. Plenty of Cabernet flavour. Much less evolved, it seems, than the 1990. Very fine quality underneath on the attack. Rich and profound if slightly austere. Good grip. More solid tannins than in the 1990 or the 1989. Slightly astringent still. It still seems as if it needs more time to mellow. Very lovely, long, cool, classy finish. Very fine indeed.
2005–25

Vintage 1982
Splendid colour. Very full. Now mature. Impressive nose. Very rich and concentrated. Very profound. Splendidly ripe. Abundant. Rich but very fresh. Very harmonious. On the palate verging on the voluptuous. Fullish body. Much smoother than the 1986. Very rich and velvety. Quite powerfully flavoured. Very lovely.
2005–20

Latour

Frédéric Engerer
director

Château Latour
St-Lambert
33250 Pauillac
Tel: +33 5 56 73 19 80
Fax: +33 5 56 73 19 81
Email: info@chateau-
latour.com
www.chateau-latour.com
red: Cabernet Sauvignon,
Merlot, Cabernet Franc,
Petit Verdot

Latour was the featured château at the annual Institute of Masters of Wine First Growth tasting held in London in January 2001.

RED WINES

CHATEAU LATOUR

Vintage 1996
Full colour. Austere nose. This has gone back into its shell. Very classy. Full body on the palate. Very lovely Cabernet fruit. Very Latour in character. Blackcurrant, blackberry, and black cherry. Intense and concentrated, and very classy. Excellent. Much better than the 1995.
2010–40

Vintage 1995
A little more colour than the 1996. Full and virile. The tannins are a little dry on the nose. A little burnt. Yet rich and cooked fruit underneath. More 1995 than Latour, in contrast to the 1996, says Frédéric Engerer. Quite brutal. Fullish body. Rather better at the end than on the nose. Rich and complex. Less classic than the 1996, but very fine for the vintage.
2008–30

Vintage 1994
Fullish, immature colour. Slightly dry, tannic, ungenerous nose. Medium-full body. Ripe, quite complex and concentrated palate. This is beginning to soften up. Not the greatest amount of grip and intensity. But the usual Latour class. Fine for the vintage.
2005–19

Vintage 1991
Very good colour. Now some maturity. Slightly undergrowthy on the nose. Aromatic and spicy on the palate. Getting soft now. Fresher and more fruity on the attack than the nose would suggest. Not a great deal of class though. Not very long. Just about ready.
2005–08

Vintage 1990
Fine colour. Still youthful. This is still a little closed on the nose. But underneath the sheer breed and concentration are really brilliant. Very exuberant. Great aromatic complexity. Marvellous Cabernet fruit. Very intense. Excellent grip. Still quite some tannin. Very, very fresh. Very, very long and complex. Super-duper. *Grand vin.*
2008–46

Vintage 1988
Fine colour. Impressive nose. Not too tannic. Still youthful nevertheless. Lovely Cabernet fruit. Medium-full body. Beautifully balanced, very ripe, almost sweet fruit. Not a bit too austere. Almost ready. Long, complex, intense, and very, very classy. Splendid for the vintage.
2005–28

Vintage 1986
Fullish colour. Fine nose. Just a bit of tannin still. Rich, but slightly austere still. Very fine fruit on the palate. Lovely ripe Cabernet. What it lacks, after the 1990, is the concentration and intensity. Good length but not the greatest grip or depth. This is fine but not great.
2005–30

Vintage 1982
Fine colour. This is now fully ready. Rich, aromatic, fat, and exotic on both nose and palate. Fullish body. Meaty. Almost sweet. Very fine fruit. Lovely lingering finish. Long, complex, and certainly very fine indeed. But I prefer the 1990.
2005–30

Three Léovilles and a château called Ducru

From top:
Anthony Barton, *proprietor*, **Léoville Barton**, 33250 St-Julien Beychevelle
Tel: +33 5 56 59 06 05;
Fax: +33 5 56 59 14 29
Email: chateau@leoville-barton.com
www.leoville-barton.com

the late Michel Delon, *manager*, **Léoville Las Cases**, 33250 St-Julien Beychevelle
Tel: +33 5 56 73 25 26;
Fax: +33 5 56 59 18 33
Email: leoville-las-cases@wanadoo.fr

Didier Cuvelier, *proprietor*, **Léoville Poyferré**, 33250 St-Julien Beychevelle
Tel: +33 5 56 59 08 30;
Fax: +33 5 56 59 60 09
Email: lp@leoville-poyferre.fr; www.leoville-poyferre.fr

Bruno Borie, *proprietor*, **Ducru-Beaucaillou**, 33250 St-Julien Beychevelle
Tel: +33 5 56 73 16 73;
Fax: +33 5 56 59 27 37
Email: je-borie@je-borie.sa.com

The following wines were tasted in New Hampshire, USA, in October 2002. My thanks to my hosts, Jack and Thelma Hewitt, and to other friends who contributed samples.

RED WINE

CHATEAU LEOVILLE BARTON
Vintage 1996
Good colour. Rich nose. Firm, classy, and backward. Some tannin. Fullish body. Ripe, well-covered tannins. Rich fruit. Good grip. Lots of class and depth, a complex, long finish. Very classic. Very promising. Fine plus.
2008–28

CHATEAU LEOVILLE LAS CASES
Vintage 1996
Good colour. Full, firm, backward, austere nose. Lots of depth underneath. A big, tannic, very concentrated wine. Splendidly rich underneath. Vigorous, powerful, intense. Excellent grip. A splendid example. Very fine plus.
2010–30+

CHATEAU LEOVILLE POYFERRE
Vintage 1996
Good colour. Rich, plump, succulent nose. More Merlot in flavour than Léoville Barton or Las Cases. Riper and more ample yet plenty of depth. On the palate this is ripe and medium–full-bodied, with well-covered tannins. Good balance, lots of seductive charm. It finishes well. Fine.
2006–26

CHATEAU DUCRU–BEAUCAILLOU
Vintage 1996
Good colour. Quite accessible, supremely elegant and harmonious nose. Medium-full body. Concentrated, lovely old viney fruit. Excellent grip. Multi-dimensional and complex on the palate. Very long. Very fine.
2006–30

CHATEAU LEOVILLE BARTON
Vintage 1995
Very good colour. Good nose, but not as rich or intense as the 1996. Medium-full body. Some tannin, but not a great deal of grip, making it as much astringent as tannic. It lacks a bit of freshness. A bad bottle? It showed much better (fine plus) at a Barton vertical in April 2001.
2005–10

CHATEAU LEOVILLE LAS CASES
Vintage 1995
Very good colour. Lovely nose. Rich, concentrated, and classic. Rather less firm and austere than the 1996. Fullish body. Finely balanced. No lack of grip. Lovely fruit. Bigger than the Ducru. Very classy. Very fine.
2005–20+

CHATEAU LEOVILLE POYFERRE
Vintage 1995
Very good colour. Ample nose. Softening now. Medium to medium-full body. Like the Barton a slight lack of grip, but more fruit and ripeness. Decent length. Very good.
2005–16

CHATEAU DUCRU–BEAUCAILLOU
Vintage 1995
Very good colour, lovely nose. Fullish, generous, classy, and harmonious. Medium-full body. Much better grip and definition than Barton or Poyferré. Elegant like the 1996. Nearly as good. Very long and lovely finish. Very fine.
2005–20+

CHATEAU LEOVILLE BARTON
Vintage 1990
Full colour. Still immature. Ripe nose. A bit adolescent. Curious. There is a vegetal taint here (stewed nettles). Fullish body on palate. Some tannin. Decent grip. Rich fruit mixed with this odd flavour. Will it go? Gets better in the glass. Quite powerful. Plenty of depth. Fine plus.
2005–23

CHATEAU LEOVILLE LAS CASES
Vintage 1990
Full colour. Still immature. Still some tannin on the nose. A firm, backward wine but a very good one. Ripe and rich. Excellent grip. Still a touch ungainly but potentially very fine. But the 1996 is better still.
2005–25

CHATEAU LEOVILLE POYFERRE
Vintage 1990
Full colour. A suggestion of maturity. Lovely ripe nose. Less adolescent than Barton or Las Cases, beginning to show well. Medium-full body. Plump, seductive, complex fruit. Harmonious, classy, and vigorous. Very fine. Better than 1995 and 1996. Just about ready.
2005–20

Margaux

Paul Pontallier
director

Château Margaux
33460 Margaux
Tel: +33 5 57 88 83 83
Fax: +33 5 57 88 31 32
Email: chateau-
margaux@chateau-
margaux.com
www.chateau-margaux.com
red: Cabernet Sauvignon,
Merlot, Cabernet Franc,
Petit Verdot

The following vintages of Château Margaux were sampled at one of my Master tastings in London in November 2002. All the wines had come direct from the château.

RED WINE

CHATEAU MARGAUX

Vintage 1996
Full colour. Still very youthful. On the nose this is still closed and even a bit clumsy for the moment. Better on the palate. Full body. Some tannin. Just a little oak. Good grip. The fruit is classy and succulent. There is plenty of concentration and the finish is ripe, complex, rich, and elegant. Very fine.
2008–28

Vintage 1995
Full colour. Still very youthful. Fresh, positive, succulent nose. Today rather more together and approachable than the 1996. On the palate this is fullish-bodied. The tannins are beginning to get absorbed. It doesn't quite have the flair and definition of the 1996 but there is lovely balanced, rich fruit here and plenty of subtlety at the end. Very fine for the vintage.
2005–20

Vintage 1990
Full colour. Still immature. Lovely nose. More clear-cut than the 1989. Full, rich, concentrated, balanced, and very complex and classy. Full-bodied on the palate. Still a little tannin. Excellent grip. Splendidly profound fruit. Excellent. Marvellous finish. A great wine.
2005–35

Vintage 1989
Fullish colour. Just about mature. Full and rich on the nose. Abundant and still a little "muddy". On the palate this is fullish-bodied. There is a little residual tannin still and the wine doesn't at present shine as much as the 1988, let alone the 1990. The finish is rich and ample and very long. Very fine for the vintage.
2005–24

Vintage 1988
Very good colour. Still fresh. Less evolved and no lighter than the 1989. Lovely nose. Ripe, balanced, relaxed, and very classy. Fullish on the palate. Lovely fresh fruit. Very elegant, very harmonious, and subtle. Long. Just about ready. Very fine indeed for the vintage. Quite delicious.
2005–20

Vintage 1986
Full colour. Less developed than the 1985. Ripe nose but a touch diffuse. Medium-full body. Decent fruit on the attack but a lack of grip, weight, and depth. Still a little unresolved tannin, which I think will always be there. The wines farther north in St-Julien and Pauillac are much better. Fine for the vintage at best.
2005–12

Vintage 1985
Very full colour. Just a hint of maturity. Softer, richer, and more positive on the nose than the 1986. Fullish body. Very ripe and succulent. Quite ready. Very good tannins. Very good grip. This is long and abundant and seductive. Lots of depth. Clearly much better than the 1986, and even the 1989, perhaps. Very fine indeed for the vintage.
2005–25

Vintage 1983
Medium-full colour. Now mature. Soft, fragrant nose. Very Margaux. Marvellously elegant. Fully ready. Medium-full-bodied, balanced, intense, and classy. Very subtle, intense, and lovely. A wine of poise and complexity. Rather lighter than the 1982 but so much more flair and depth. Very, very long. Splendid quality. For those looking for intensity and class rather than muscle. Excellent.
2005–20

Vintage 1982
Very full colour. Still youthful. Muscular on the nose. Quite some oak and quite some extraction. Much bigger than the 1983, as it always was. Still a bit of unresolved tannin. Will this go? I think not. It will always be a bit burly. Rich, fat, and opulent nevertheless. A big wine with a lot of depth. But does the 1985, let alone the 1983, have more class and better balance? Fine plus. But not great for a 1982.
2005–25

Vintage 1978
Fine, full colour. Now mature but still vigorous. Ripe and fresh on the nose. Medium-full body. This is poised and very elegant, with lovely fruit. Still very youthful on the palate. Very well balanced. Long and really succulent for a 1978. A very fine example. The wine of the vintage?
2005–20+

Palmer

Thomas Duroux, Bernard de Laage, Philippe Delfaut, *general manager, development manager, technical director*

Château Palmer
334560 Margaux
Tel: +33 5 57 88 72 72
Fax: +33 5 57 88 37 16
Email: chateau-palmer@chateau-palmer.com
www.chateau-palmer.com
red: Cabernet Sauvignon, Merlot, Petit Verdot

I offered the following range at one of my Master tastings in London in January 2002. All the wines had come direct from the château.

RED WINE

CHATEAU PALMER

Vintage 1996
Full colour. More profound than the 1995 and less advanced. Lovely rich nose. Very elegant, poised fruit. Vigorous and harmonious. Sophisticated tannins in the background. This is very promising. Full, concentrated, profound, and full of class. Lovely balance. Fine at the end. But this is going to be very fine.
2007–30+

Vintage 1995
Medium-full colour. Just a hint of development. A little tough and dry on the nose still. The tannins are a touch solid. Medium-full body. Good fruit. Ripe and with very good grip. Not quite the concentration or finesse, especially at the tannic end, of the 1996. But it finishes better than it starts. Long. Fine.
2005–22

Vintage 1990
Surprisingly, less depth of colour than not only the 1989 but the 1988. The nose is not as impressive as I had expected. Ample and fruity but without a lot of vigour and depth. Medium body on the palate. Soft, sweet, and quite forward. Balanced, fruity, and elegant but a little superficial. Yet not short. Ready now. A bit disappointing.
2005–15+

Vintage 1989
Good immature, full colour. Rich, closed-in, slightly adolescent nose. No undue density. Just taking its time to come round. Lots of depth on the palate. Still some tannin. But rich and sophisticated. Very good grip. Long and lovely. This is very fine.
2005–24

Vintage 1988
Very fine colour for the vintage. Full and vigorous. Fragrant nose. Very Palmer. Fresh. Good pure fruit. Complex. But medium-full body rather than very full. Just about ready. More slightly raw than with unresolved tannins. Good acidity. Very fresh, classy fruit. Not the depth and concentration of the 1989 but fine plus for the vintage. It will last well.
2005–20+

Vintage 1986
Good full colour. Barely mature. Just a little solid on the nose. Still some tannin. But ripe and rich underneath. Better on the palate. Very good concentrated fruit and very good grip. No undue tannic structure. Full body. Old viney creaminess. This has lots of depth and lots of definition. Vigorous. Better than the 1989. Better acidity and more sheer breed. A lovely example. Just about there. Very fine.
2005–30

Vintage 1985
Mature, fullish colour. Soft, aromatic, classy, and seductive on the nose. Now mature and velvety. This is in total contrast to the 1986 but equally good. Medium-full body. Now round and even mellow. Splendidly complete and harmonious. Great subtlety and class. It doesn't have the size of the 1986 but it has lots of dimension and complexity. Very long. Lovely finish. Very fine.
2005–20+

Vintage 1983
Fullish colour. Less evolved than the 1982. Fuller, firmer, and less evolved on the nose than the 1982. Fresh but not exactly voluptuous. Medium-full body on the palate. Clean and classy. Lovely fruit. Fully ready. Slightly less concentrated than the 1985 and the 1982, but beautifully balanced. Very long and very impressive. More positive at the end than the 1982 if not as seductive. Very fine.
2005–20+

Vintage 1982
Fullish colour. Now mature – more so than the 1983. Rich and ripe. Mellow and concentrated. Fullish and abundant on the nose. This is very lovely and very 1982. Sweet, creamy, round, and fat. Very good concentration. Very good acidity too. But no hard edges now. Velvety on the palate. Voluptuous, harmonious, classy and long. Impressive even, in a 1982 context. Very fine.
2005–20+

Pétrus

Christian Moueix
director

Château Pétrus
33500 Pomerol
Tel: Unavailable
Fax: Unavailable
red: Merlot, Cabernet Franc

The following vintages of Château Pétrus were shown at a Masters of Wine tasting presented by Christian Moueix in London in January 2004.

RED WINE

CHATEAU PETRUS

Vintage 2000
Fine colour. Full, rich, substantial nose. Not too dense. Very Merlot. Mulberry as it developed. Well-integrated oak. Lovely fruit. Very concentrated. Very relaxed. Full-bodied but not overpoweringly so. Excellent grip, great depth and intensity. Lovely fruit and class. Harmonious and very, very long. Very, very lovely. An explosion of flavour. A little more powerful than the 1998.
2015–45

Vintage 1999
Fullish colour. Fresh on the nose. Attractive fruit and a touch of spice as it developed. No lack of style. Medium body on the palate. Good balance. Decent length. Not a lot of tannin, quite floral. Charming and positive at the end. Very good for the vintage.
2006–16

Vintage 1998
Fine, full, youthful colour. Fresh on the nose, with a slight touch of mocha. Pure, intense, rich, and complex. Fullish body. Very good tannins. Powerful. Good grip. Perfect maturity here. Beautifully elegant – even more so than the 2000. Splendidly harmonious. A great wine.
2013–45

Vintage 1995
Fine colour. Still immature but showing a little brown at the rim. On the nose a little adolescent. The tannins show a little. Ripe Merlot with a slight austerity. On the palate this is fullish-bodied. Slightly astringent at present but only on the attack. Rich, quite concentrated, balanced, and elegant on the follow-through. It became more civilized and rounder. Slight cedar-woody touches. Very fine, but not as great as the 1998.
2007–27

Vintage 1990
Full colour. Still youthful. Very ample, ripe, plummy character on the nose. But very fresh. Full-bodied and vigorous on the palate. Still a little unresolved tannin. Excellent grip. Lots of depth and dimension. Rich, fat but fresh and complex at the end. Very lovely. Sweeter, richer, and more seductive than the 1989 today.
2006–30

Vintage 1989
Full colour. Slightly more evolved than the 1990. Richer, sweeter, and more spicy on the nose than the 1990. Slightly drier. Fullish body. A little astringent rather than a lot of tannic structure. Slightly less volume than the 1990 and a much more spicy flavour. I prefer the 1990 today. This has aspects of the Midi, but is still very youthful.
2006–30

Vintage 1982
Ample, voluptuous, ripe Merlot nose. Lots of depth. Still vigorous, rich, and energetic. Very, very complex. Full-bodied, velvety, and very fresh still. Marvellous depth. Beautifully poised. Very long. Very round but very vigorous. A brilliant example.
2005–18+

Vintage 1978
Medium-full colour. Now some age, especially compared with the 1982. Cool on the nose. Slightly austere. But good class. "Rosewater," says Christian Moueix. Medium–full-bodied on the palate. Round. A naturally sweet finish. A delightful bottle. Very classy. Much more charm on the palate than on the nose.
drink soon

Trotanoy

Christian Moueix
director (see left)

Château Trotanoy
33500 Pomerol
Tel: Unavailable
Fax: Unavailable
red: Merlot, Cabernet Franc

The following vintages were sampled in London at one of my Master tastings in April 2002. All the wines had come direct from the château.

RED WINE

CHATEAU TROTANOY

Vintage 1998

Full colour. Lovely rich, succulent nose. Lots of depth. Very high-class fruit. Fullish body. Very good tannins. Splendidly ample and lush. Very good grip. Long and complex. Utterly seductive! Really very fine.

2006–26

Vintage 1995

Full colour. The nose is a little hidden after the puppy-fat of the 1998. But nevertheless less ripe, rich, and sophisticated. Fullish body. Balanced, seductive, fresh, and fragrant. Almost as good as the 1998. Not far different in style. Very, very long. Very, very lovely. Very fine.

2005–24

Vintage 1990

Fullish colour with a touch of brown at the rim. Rich and voluptuous on the nose. Properly evolved now. Very Merlot. Medium-full body. Good ripe tannins. Good freshness. Subtle. Elegant. Fully ready. Long. Fine.

2005–15

Vintage 1989

Fullish colour with a touch of brown at the rim. Like the 1990 rich and voluptuous on the nose. But slightly less zip. Slightly drier tannins and the tannins are more obvious. A certain firmness and astringency from these tannins on the palate. But full and with more grip and depth on the palate than the 1990. More vigour. Rich at the end. Just about ready. Fine plus.

2005–20

Vintage 1988

Fullish, still quite youthful colour. Fresh nose. Just a touch vegetal after the 1990 and 1989. Medium to medium-full body. Nicely fresh. Now fully ready. Good tannins. Not lean on the palate. Fragrant, elegant, and delicious. Great charm. Very fine for the vintage.

2005–12

Vintage 1982

Full, mature colour. Splendidly rich, fullish, voluptuous nose. Real depth and dimension. Full body. Multi-dimensional. Excellent grip. Really rich. This has real depth and complexity. A marvellous example. Very fine even within the context of the vintage. Ready but will keep for ages.

2005–18

Vintage 1979

Fullish, mature colour but no sign of age. Well mature, slightly dried-up nose. Fresher as it evolved. Medium body. Plump and fresh. Elegant and fruity. Good length. But a little more one-dimensional compared with the 1978. Fine for the vintage at the very least though.

2005–08

Vintage 1978

Medium-full colour. Less vigorous-looking than the 1979. More developed too. Soft and fragrant but very classy on the nose. Splendid but slightly delicate fruit. Medium body. No more than the 1979. More depth and dimension though. Fresher. Lovely fruit. A gentle wine but by no means short. Complex, subtle, and delicious at the end. Fine plus.

2005–12

BURGUNDY

Anne Gros

Anne-Françoise Gros
proprietor

Domaine Anne Gros
11 rue des Communes
21700 Vosne-Romanée
Tel: +33 3 80 61 07 95
Fax: +33 3 80 61 23 21
www.anne-gros.com
red: Pinot Noir

I sampled Anne Gros's Richebourg wines in Vosne-Romanée in February 2004. The Domaine Anne & François Gros wines are from the time when Anne made wine with her father, François.

RED WINE

RICHEBOURG

Vintage 2002, Domaine Anne Gros
Medium-full colour. Bottled two months previously. Lovely soft red fruit nose. Medium to fullish body on the palate. Very good grip. The tannins are soft and ripe. This is potentially very lush and succulent, but by no means a blockbuster. Very seductive. Very fine.
2011–25

Vintage 2001, Domaine Anne Gros
New label. Medium-full colour. This has gone into its shell a little on the nose. Medium-full body. More obviously tannic structure than the 2002. Very good grip. Slightly less rich. Certainly less plump. But more spice. Plenty of energy and distinction. Lovely long, complex finish. Very fine.
2011–25

Vintage 2000, Domaine Anne Gros
Surprisingly good colour. Soft nose. A little light but no lack of fruit, elegance, harmony, or succulence. Medium to medium-full body. This is excellent for the vintage. Surprisingly voluminous. Fresh and balanced. Ripe and classy. Very lovely.
2012–42

Vintage 1999, Domaine Anne Gros
Very fine colour. Marvellous nose. Full, concentrated, rich, profound, very elegant, and complex. Still very young. Full body. Excellent grip. Very concentrated. Very fine tannins. This is clearly superior to the more recent vintages. Splendid fruit. Very, very long and multi-dimensional. A great wine!
2012–42

Vintage 1998, Domaine Anne Gros
Very good colour. Just a suggestion of brown. Fullish nose. Rich, exotic, and spicy. A touch of caramel and mocha at present. Cedary flavours as it developed. Fullish body. Some tannin. Very good acidity. Nice ripe, cool fruit on the palate. Plenty of substance and depth. It needs to be kept while the tannins soften up. Very fine.
2010–30

Vintage 1997, Domaine Anne Gros
Medium-full colour. Some maturity. Soft nose. Just a little diffuse after the 1998 and 1996. Medium to medium-full body. Ripe and quite fresh. But a little weak. It lacks bite. Nevertheless very good indeed if not fine within the context of this vintage. Ultimately unfortunately it lacks depth and dimension. Ready.
2005–07

Vintage 1996, Domaine Anne Gros
Fine colour. Still very youthful. Rather austere on the nose. Even a slightly vegetal, lean touch. Is it always going to be a bit like this, I wondered. On the palate though much more round and generous. Full body. Still some tannin to round off. High acidity keeping it fresh. Long and stylish. This is very fine indeed.
2008–30

Vintage 1995, Domaine Anne Gros
The first vintage with simply Anne Gros on the label. Very fine colour. Just a hint of maturity. Rich, full, profound nose. A full-bodied wine. Plenty of structure but not too solid or tannic. Full and youthful. Still quite a lot of tannin to be absorbed, more than the 1996, but it is rounder, fatter, and richer as well. Not quite so elegant, perhaps. Like the 1996, emphatically a wine for food. But not yet.
2008–25

Vintage 1993, Domaine Anne & François Gros
Very fine colour. Only a suggestion of maturity. Rich, concentrated, intensely flavoured nose. A great deal of depth here. And dimension too. On the palate this is beginning to get there. Full body. Very fine grip. Just a little unresolved tannin. Very, very lovely, cool, complex fruit. Long and very lovely indeed. Very pure. This is a great wine. Clearly superior to 1995.
2008–50

Vintage 1990, Domaine Anne & François Gros
Very full colour. Still very youthful-looking. Splendidly rich nose. Fresh chocolate, cooked plum tart, and black cherry. Full but getting round. Exotic. Fullish body. Just about ready but keeping it a year or two more would be no bad idea. It will get really velvety. Balanced, rich, cool and stylish. Not as great as the 1993, but still very fine.
2005–25

Armand Rousseau

Charles Rousseau
proprietor

Domaine Armand Rousseau
1 rue de l'Aumônerie
Tel: +33 3 80 34 30 55
Fax: +33 3 80 58 50 25
Email: contact@domaine-
rousseau.com
www.domaine-
rousseau.com
red: Pinot Noir

The following wines were sampled in London in December 2002.

RED WINES

GEVREY–CHAMBERTIN, CLOS ST-JACQUES
Vintage 1996
Good colour. Full, firm, and rich. More austere than 1995. Fullish body. Good grip. Lots of class and depth, and energy. Long and classy. Lovely complex fruit. Very fine.
2005–18

CHAMBERTIN, CLOS DE BEZE
Vintage 1996
Less firm than the Clos St-Jacques. Ripe and ample and aromatic. Fullish-bodied and rich on the palate. Not quite the vigour or grip of the Clos St-Jacques. Plenty of acidity on the follow-through. More definition at end. Fine plus.
2005–16

LE CHAMBERTIN
Vintage 1996
Lovely rich nose. Very well-covered tannins. Clearly the best of the 1996s. Very classy. Full-bodied and concen-trated. Excellent fruit. Vigorous. Still a little tannin to resolve. Very long and complex. An aristocrat. Excellent.
2006–20+

GEVREY–CHAMBERTIN, CLOS ST-JACQUES
Vintage 1995
Good colour. Rich, spicy, exotic nose. Even a touch of sweetness. Fullish body. Ripe and flamboyant. Slightly red fruity. Good vigorous attack. Good grip on the follow-through. Lots of depth. Very fine.
2006–20

CHAMBERTIN, CLOS DE BEZE
Vintage 1995
Again a splendid rich, ripe nose. Slightly less concen-trated and less grip. Plenty of fruit. Good acidity. Ample. *A point*. Fine.
2005–15

LE CHAMBERTIN
Vintage 1995
Good colour. Classic nose. Lots of blackcurrant. Much less spicy than the Clos de Bèze. Most impressive, if young, with tannin to resolve. Concentrated. Good grip. Lots of substance here. Lovely fruit and length. Splendid.
2007–20+

GEVREY–CHAMBERTIN, CLOS ST-JACQUES
Vintage 1993
Very good colour. Slightly closed-in on the nose but great depth. Classy fruit. Fullish body with concentration and grip. Splendid individuality. More dimension than either the 1996 or 1995. Will last for ages. Very fine.
2005–25

CHAMBERTIN, CLOS DE BEZE
Vintage 1993
Very good colour. Firm nose. Some tannin. Rich but closed. Lots of depth and concentration if slightly adolescent. Richer than the Clos St-Jacques. Full body. Fat, rich, exotic, and flamboyant. Splendid depth. Lovely.
2006–30

LE CHAMBERTIN
Vintage 1993
Very good colour. Very fine nose. Like the 1995, very clean and clear-cut. Nothing but very classy fruit and a lot of depth and complexity. Marvellously pure and rich. A full-bodied wine with an aristocratic, multi-dimensional character. Very long and complex at the end. *Grand vin*.
2006–30+

GEVREY–CHAMBERTIN, CLOS ST-JACQUES
Vintage 1990
Good colour. Rich, aromatic nose. A little tannin still. Fullish body. Still a little tannin on the palate too. Ripe, quite cooked fruit flavours. Good acidity. Plump and ripe. Lots of character and depth. Fine plus.
2005–20

CHAMBERTIN, CLOS DE BEZE
Vintage 1990
Very good colour. More sophisticated on the nose than the Clos St-Jacques. Full body. Good tannins. Splendidly vigorous, rich, and once again flamboyant. Excellent grip. Very, very lovely finish. Very fine indeed.
2005–30

LE CHAMBERTIN
Vintage 1990
Very good colour. Great purity, great class on the nose. Full-bodied and rich and complex, with lovely, splendidly abundant fruit. Great grip. Aristocratic. Great wine!
2005–30

Comte Georges de Vogüé

Jean-Luc Pépin and François Millet
*commercial director
and winemaker*

Domaine Comte Georges
de Vogüé
21220 Chambolle-Musigny
Tel: +33 3 80 62 86 25
Fax: +33 3 80 62 82 38
red: Pinot Noir

The following range of de Vogüé wines was sampled at one of my
Master tastings in May 2002.

RED WINES

CHAMBOLLE–MUSIGNY, LES AMOUREUSES
Vintage 1998
Good, fresh-looking colour. Very lovely, pure, elegant,
fragrant Pinot on the nose. Medium-full body. Gently
oaky. Still a little tannin to resolve. Just a touch bitter
at present. Lovely ample fruit though. Very good acidity.
Ripe, stylish, and very lovely. Very fine for the vintage.
2008–28

BONNES MARES
Vintage 1997
Fullish colour. Now a little sign of maturity. Quite firm
nose for a 1997. Rich. Very good acidity. Medium-full
body. A little tannin still on the palate. Good cool fruit.
Lots of elegance. Long and complex. Very fine.
2005–20

MUSIGNY, VIEILLES VIGNES
Vintage 1997
Fullish colour. Now a little sign of maturity. Softer
nose than the Bonnes Mares but more intense.
A little adolescent at present, although ripe and
complete. Medium-full body. Plenty of substance.
Lovely fruit. Very, very long at the end. Very fine
indeed for the vintage.
2006–20

CHAMBOLLE–MUSIGNY, LES AMOUREUSES
Vintage 1996
Good colour. Still youthful. Very lovely nose. Intense,
ripe, harmonious, and profound. On the palate still a
little tannin. Fullish body. Excellent grip. Real intensity
and dimension on the follow-through. Really delicious.
Very long. Very elegant. Very fine.
2006–25

BONNES MARES
Vintage 1996
Full colour. Still very young. Rather more muscular on
the nose than the Amoureuses. Fat and rich. Fullish
weight on the palate. Abundant fruit. Good acidity. Still
some tannin. Most impressive at the end. Marvellously
intense, classy finish. It goes on and on. Very fine plus.
2008–38

MUSIGNY, VIEILLES VIGNES
Vintage 1996
Even more youthful colour than the Bonnes Mares
1996. A little closed-in on the nose. Fullish body.
Multi-dimensional flavours. A little tannin. Marvellous
grip. Great breed. Totally aristocratic. Magnificent!
2008–38

CHAMBOLLE–MUSIGNY, LES AMOUREUSES
Vintage 1993
Very good colour. Rich, full, and very delicious on
the nose. Full-bodied, fat, and gently oaky. Still some
tannin. More structured as well as more concentrated
than the 1996. Very intense. Really quite powerful,
yet very composed and classy. Excellent fruit. Fine grip.
Brilliant. Very fine.
2006–25

BONNES MARES
Vintage 1993
Similarly very good colour to the Amoureuses. Denser on
the nose. Still a bit closed and adolescent. Splendid on the
palate. Rather more black fruity. Fullish body. Still some
tannins, but they are ripe and fat. I think I prefer the flair
and dimension of the Amoureuses, but this is very fine.
2007–35

MUSIGNY
Vintage 1993
Marvellously deep, rich colour. Still very young, quite
closed on the nose. Fullish body. A complete, multi-
dimensional wine. Still hidden. It is the Bonnes Mares
which sings today. But this is potentially great – up to
1990 levels. Utterly brilliant fruit. Very long. Splendid.
2008–35

MUSIGNY
Vintage 1990
Similarly splendid, deep colour to the 1993, but more
advanced. All sorts of 1990 aromas on the nose. Caramel,
leather, liquorice, and mocha. Very rich and sweet. Very
full-bodied. The tannins are getting soft. Excellent acidity.
Really, very concentrated. Beginning to come out of its
adolescent period. Marvellous quality. Very, very long and
multi-dimensional at the end. A truly great wine.
2005–35

Comtes Lafon

Dominique Lafon
proprietor

Domaine des Comtes Lafon
Clos de la Barre
21190 Meursault
Tel: +33 3 80 21 22 17
Fax: +33 3 80 21 61 64
Email: comtes.lafon@
wanadoo.fr
www.comtes.lafon.fr
white: Chardonnay

The following wines were presented at one of my Master tastings in London
in May 2002.

WHITE WINES

MEURSAULT
Vintage 1997
Ripe, rich but slightly adolescent nose. Less so on the
palate. Juicy and succulent. Clean, balanced, and fullish.
Lots of depth and style. Excellent for a village example.
Lovely pure fruit. Will still get better.
2005–10

MEURSAULT, PERRIERES
Vintage 1996
Very fine, full, rich nose. Very good acidity of course,
but lots of concentration. Full on the palate. Really very
fine depth and complexity. Very youthful. But already
very impressive. Cool, complex, rich, and pure. Very
lovely. Very, very long on the palate. Very fine plus.
2005–14+

Vintage 1995
Splendid nose. Very high class. Very fine acidity. Fresh
and very, very concentrated indeed. Marvellous depth
of flavour here. This is still a bit adolescent on the
palate. Multi-dimensional. Excellent grip. A simply
splendid example. Marvellous finish.
2005–18+

Vintage 1994
Broad flavoured, mature, gently oaky nose. Good
freshness. Medium body. Good complexity for the
vintage. But not the dimension of most of the 1990s
vintages. Plump, ripe, balanced, and charming. Good
positive finish. Fine for the vintage.
2005–08

Vintage 1993
Fuller but slightly leaner on the nose than the 1994.
More concentrated. Greater acidity. Medium-full body
on the palate. Good oak. Very lovely peachy fruit. Not
a bit lean on the follow-through. Not the depth of the
1992 but much more interesting than the 1994. Lots
of charm. Very long and complex. Now ready but no
hurry to drink. Very fine for the vintage.
2005–10

Vintage 1992
A mature colour now. Evolved, complex, spicy nose.
Fully mature. Getting nutty but still the mineral aspect
and the floweriness predominate. Full and concentrated
though. And good grip. Rather more to it than the
1993 as well as richer. This has the saving grace of
both backbone and acidity. Lots of wine here. Will
still improve, I can't help feeling. Certainly bags of life.
Very concentrated and complex. Very classy. Excellent
finish. Very fine plus.
2005–12+

MEURSAULT, CHARMES
Vintage 1990
Youthful colour. Fresh, flowery, youthful nose. Ripe.
Good acidity. Classy and complex. Fullish, peachy,
and gently oaky. Ripe and rich and splendidly balanced.
Very, very lovely, and complex at the end. *A point* but
will last well. Very fine.
2005–10+

MEURSAULT, GENEVRIERES
Vintage 1990
A more evolved colour than the Charmes. A little
oxidation on the nose. Not too bad on the palate.
Ripe, nutty, and full-bodied. Good acidity. Slightly
citrussy. Not the depth of the Charmes or sheer
style and magic of the Perrières 1990. But, despite
the nose, still enjoyable. Very good.
drink soon

MEURSAULT, PERRIERES
Vintage 1990
Some evolution on the colour. Very full on the nose –
much fuller than the Charmes. Concentrated. Lots
and lots of depth and dimension. Very impressive.
Full body. Excellent grip. *A point* and very delicious.
Rich, harmonious, profound, and multi-dimensional.
Very, very long. Excellent. Burgundy doesn't come
much better than this!
2005–10+

Joseph Drouhin

Robert Drouhin
proprietor

Maison Joseph Drouhin
7 rue d'Enfer
21201 Beaune
Tel: +33 3 80 24 68 88
Fax: +33 3 80 22 43 14
Email: maisondrouhin@
drouhin.com
www.drouhin.com
red: Pinot Noir

The following Griottes were sampled at one of my Master Tastings in July 2003.

RED WINE

GRIOTTE–CHAMBERTIN

Vintage 1999
Good full colour. Rich, intensely concentrated and very harmonious. Very lovely ripe, classy fruit here on the nose. Good tannins. Very good acidity. A little austere at present. But a lot of depth and interest. Very long. Fine plus – perhaps even better.
2010–30

Vintage 1998
Good full colour. Now with some signs of maturity. A broader, slightly more loose-knit fruit flavour on the nose. No hard tannins though. Smooth, ripe, and slightly caramel spiced. Medium-full body. Rich, fat, and quite meaty. Good grip. This is a lovely example. Very long. Lots of depth. Very fine for the vintage.
2008–24

Vintage 1996
Medium-full colour. Still youthful. Classy nose, but slightly lean. Yet plenty of ripe, fresh, balanced fruit. Medium-full body. Lots of class. Plenty of depth. Very long and complex at the end. Very pure. It needs time to round off and become more generous. But fine plus/very fine again.
2008–26

Vintage 1995
Fullish colour. A touch of brown at the rim. Full, rich, meaty nose. Plenty of depth and not unduly tannic. Full-bodied, rich, and admirable. Not a bit too much bulk. Good grip. Plenty of depth. Very good concentration on the follow-through. Very fine. Better than the 1996 perhaps.
2008–26

Vintage 1993
Fullish colour. Little sign of maturity. Rich, full, potentially opulent nose. Still a little closed. Lots of depth and concentration. Lots of class. Full-bodied, ample, rich, intense, and very well balanced on the palate. Very good tannins. Lots of vigour and depth. Excellent long finish. This is very lovely. Multi-dimensional. Very fine.
2006–26

Vintage 1991
Medium-full, mature colour. Lovely, just about mature Pinot on the nose. Ripe, abundant, and with plenty of depth. Medium-full body. Balanced, classy, fresh, and lovely. This is now *à point* but has plenty of vigour. Good concentration and dimension. Lovely long finish. Very fine for the vintage.
2005–16

Vintage 1989
Medium-full, mature colour. Ripe, opulent, sweet, and seductive on the nose. Lovely rich fruit here. Medium-full body. Rich. *A point*. Very lovely fruit. Classier than the 1991 and longer and with more dimension on the follow-through. Surprisingly good acidity. Lots of concentration. Very lovely and seductive. Will keep well.
2005–18

Vintage 1985
Fullish colour. Properly mature. Rich, vigorous, opulent, and classy on the nose. Very lovely fruit here. Splendidly balanced. Fullish-bodied, plump, and *à point*. Fresh for a 1985. Very smooth and silky. This is a lot better than the 1989. Very, very lovely. Everything in place. Very, very long. Lovely lingering, complex finish. Excellent. Will last well.
2005–20

Vintage 1976
Fullish colour. Surprisingly purple, especially for the vintage. Fresh, vigorous nose. Complex spices. Very good fruit. Very lovely. On the palate a meaty wine. But plenty of class and very good grip. Medium-full body. The tannins are now soft. Not a bit astringent. Very good acidity. This is surprisingly good. Slightly four-square but that is the 1976 vintage.
2005–10

Leflaive

Anne-Claude Leflaive
proprietor

Domaine Leflaive
Place du Monument
21190 Puligny-Montrachet
Tel: +33 3 80 21 30 13
Fax: +33 3 80 21 39 57
Email: contact@leflaive.fr
www.leflaive.fr
white: Chardonnay

I sampled the following wines at the domaine in February 2004.

WHITE WINE

CHEVALIER-MONTRACHET

Vintage 2002
Medium colour. Still very young. Rich, full, abundant, and quite powerful on the nose. Full body. Lots of depth. Slightly shaken up because it had recently been fined, but lots of substance on the follow-though. Fine grip. Lots of classy fruit. Very promising. Very fine for the vintage.
2010–25

Vintage 2001
Medium colour. Refined, much more developed than the 2002 on the nose. Lighter, of course, but no lack of fruit and depth. Ripe. Medium to medium-full body. Balanced and stylish. A lot of dimension and personality for a 2001. Lovely finish. Very fine for the vintage.
2007–20

Vintage 2000
Medium colour. Very lovely nose. Still youthful. A marvellous mix of white peaches, flowers, and a gentle touch of oak. Fullish-bodied. Vigorous. Well balanced and concentrated. Pure. Profound. This is very fine indeed.
2010–25

Vintage 1999
Medium colour. More closed-in but richer, nuttier, and fuller on the nose than the 2000. More volume and depth, less high tones. Fuller and more concentrated than the 2000 on the palate. Even more depth and dimension. Excellent fruit. Lovely balance. Yet more class and definition. A great wine!
2010–30

Vintage 1998
The colour is more evolved. Quite a lot more advanced than the 2000 and the 1999. A touch herbal and attenuated on the nose. Medium weight. Good depth and freshness on the palate, but it is outclassed by its successors. Plump, ripe, and positive at the end. This is very fine for the vintage, but not developing very well. A small harvest as a result of April frost helped the quality.
2006–18

Vintage 1997
Youthful colour. Fresher on the nose than the 1998. Balanced. Plump. Stylish. Just about ready. Medium weight. Better than the 1998 and fine for a 1997. Lots of depth, class, and definition. Very well balanced, fresh, and positive. Clean, pure, and minerally. Very long at the end.
2005–12

Vintage 1996
The 1996s were bottled very late (July 1998) as the malolactic fermentations finished in tank, not in cask. Just a little development on the nose. A full, firm, slightly austere and heavy nose. Quite high acidity. A big, intense wine. But for me it lacks a little class compared with the 1997, let alone 1999 and 2000. A little reduction. Doesn't sing today. Are other bottles different?
2006–12

Vintage 1995
Similar colour to the 1996. Just a little development. Discreet. Profound. Complex and classy on the nose. Full body. Lovely balance. Intensely flavoured. Rich but not a big wine. Lovely fruit. Not as fine in its context as 1999 and 2000. Lingering finish. Very fine indeed but not great.
2005–15+

Vintage 1993
Good colour. Plenty of quality here on the nose. Quite concentrated with class and depth. Full body. Minerally and slightly austere. This is what the 1996 should have been. Closed-in, youthful, steely. Very much to my taste. Highly original. Lots of life ahead of it. Great with food.
2005–15+

Vintage 1992
Really quite alcoholic, but it doesn't show too obviously. Slightly more evolution on the colour than the 1993, but still very fresh. Floral nose. Medium-full body. No lack of grip on the palate. A wine of fruit salad and flowers. Succulent, rich, and elegant. Long and positive. It won't last like the 1993 but it can safely be kept. Lots of charm.
2005–10

Vintage 1990
A fresh, ripe, discreet, mineral nose. Medium-full. Rich, classy fruit. Very well balanced. This has a lot of depth and intensity and is still youthful. Very fine indeed. Will last very well indeed.
2005–15+

Leroy

Lalou Bize-Leroy
proprietor

Domaine Leroy
15 rue de la Fontaine
21700 Vosne-Romanée
Tel: +33 3 80 21 21 10
Fax: +33 3 80 21 63 81
www.domaine-leroy.com
red: Pinot Noir

I tasted the following vintages of Romanée-St-Vivant in Burgundy in April 2000.

RED WINE

ROMANEE-ST-VIVANT

Vintage 1998
Medium-full colour. Lush, concentrated, and cedary on the nose. Very classy. Very seductive. Fullish structure. Balanced and very succulent. A very lovely example. Very ripe tannins. But not the structure of 1995 or 1996. Yet intense, long, and lovely. Fine plus.
2005–18

Vintage 1997
Quite a lot less colour than the 1995/1996. More developed too. On the palate it is medium-full-bodied. Very lovely ripe fruit at first but the after-taste doesn't quite live up to this. Lovely though. Juicy and very well balanced. Seductive.
2005–12

Vintage 1996
Full colour. Slightly more than the 1995. Splendid nose. Fresh and very concentrated. A slight touch of mint. Full, concentrated, and tannic on the palate. Marvellous fruit. Excellent grip. This is intense and brilliant. Great length. Very fine indeed. Best of the series.
2008–24+

Vintage 1995
Full colour. Full, rich, and fat on the nose. None of the stems of the 1993. Full, fat, spicier than the 1996. Not quite as classy or as sublime. But excellent grip. A long, fine follow-through. Very fine fruit. A very lovely wine.
now–2018

Vintage 1994
Medium to medium-full colour. Fully mature. Soft, round, ample, ripe nose. Not a great deal of weight and structure. But fresh and attractive. A marvellous 1994. Full and rich and plenty of definition. Fullish body. Balanced. Very fine. Give it another year or so.
2005–10

Vintage 1993
Fullish colour. Some development. Firm nose. You can find the stems. Still very youthful. Slightly raw and fiery. Medium-full body. Very good grip but a little lean. It lacks the fat of the 1996. And the ripeness. It reminds me a little of Côte-Rôtie. Very fine indeed though.
2005–18

Vintage 1992
Medium-full, mature colour. Ample, fat nose. No lack of substance. A slight touch of reduction. Ripe, even sweet on the palate. Fullish body. Good tannins. The attack is fresh. This is very fine for the vintage. Just about ready.
2005–08

Vintage 1991
Medium-full colour but not much sign of maturity. Fullish, rich, balanced, sophisticated nose. Fullish body. Ample and spicy. Good tannins. Fine finish. Lovely fruit. *A point*. This is very fine indeed for the vintage.
2005–11+

Vintage 1990
Fine, full, youthful colour. Very fine nose. Splendid depth and essence of fruit. Full, concentrated, and tannic. Very good grip yet an aspect of chocolate and cooked fruit. Plenty of fat here. Will still improve. Very fine. But not quite the flair for great.
2005–15

Vintage 1989
Medium to medium-full colour. Much looser-knit looking than the 1990. Round, ripe, sweet but without the structure and vigour of the 1990. Medium-full body. Fresh, ripe, and succulent. But it lacks the weight and thrust of the 1990. Very fine for the vintage but not great.
2005–11+

Louis Jadot

Pierre-Henri Gagey
director

Domaine Louis Jadot
21 rue Eugène Spuller
21203 Beaune
Tel: +33 3 80 22 10 57
Fax: +33 3 80 22 56 03
Email: contact@louisjadot.com
www.louisjadot.com
red: Pinot Noir

The following wines were offered at a wine weekend, presented by Pierre-Henri Gagey, at the Studley Priory Hotel, Oxfordshire, in November 2002.

RED WINE

GEVREY-CHAMBERTIN, CLOS ST-JACQUES

Vintage 1999
Medium-full colour. Ripe, concentrated, virile, classy nose. Marvellous purity and perfume. Still youthful, but quite approachable. Has not yet gone into its shell. Fullish body. Abundant, succulent, and balanced. Very well-covered tannin. Very good grip. Profound and concentrated. Classy and very fine.
2009–29

Vintage 1998
Medium-full colour. Quite nutty on the nose with a little touch of reduction. Not as succulent as the 1999. Slightly tougher than the 1999. The tannins are more evident. Fullish body. Good grip. Plenty of richness if not the depth and concentration of 1999. But it is slightly more adolescent. A very promising wine. Fine plus for the vintage.
2007–23

Vintage 1997
Medium-full colour. Now a touch of brown. Fresh, aromatic nose. Not a lot of depth. Forward and fruity. Round and ripe. Medium-full body. Good acidity. Not a lot of backbone, of course. But not a bit short and no lack of freshness. Easy to enjoy. Ready.
2005–14

Vintage 1996
Full colour. Fuller than the 1999 and 1998 today. Quite full, firm, very fresh nose. Very classy. Good fresh, fruity attack. Medium-full body. Not quite the concentration and intensity of 1996s in Vosne-Romanée. Reasonably forward. Lovely stylish finish. For the vintage, fine but not great.
2005–18

Vintage 1995
Full colour. Adolescent nose. A little sulphur dioxide. Fullish body. Quite some tannin, and a little astringent. This doesn't really sing today. There is good fruit and grip. But a slight lack of class. Ungainly. A second bottle was cleaner and with rather more definition. No sulphur dioxide. A big wine. Juicy, ripe, balanced, and quite structured. Lovely long finish. Very fine.
2006–24

Vintage 1993
Fine colour. Slight peppermint flavour on the nose. Firm, closed, full, and concentrated on both nose and palate. This is a backward wine still. A touch adolescent but it promises very well. Slightly austere. But very high quality. Very lovely at the end. Real personality. Still needs three or four years to soften. High-class perfumes. The tannins are not a bit aggressive. Very fine.
2005–25

Vintage 1990
Full, rich, mature colour. Lovely rich, chocolatey nose. Very aromatic. Quite substantial. Full body on the palate. Creamy-rich. Very concentrated. Only just about ready. Good vigour. Good grip. Good intensity. Lovely abundant follow-through. Very fine.
2005–25

Vintage 1985
Medium-full, rich, well-matured colour. Aromatic, fragrant, old-vine burgundy on the nose. Medium-full body. *A point*. Properly sensual. Sweet, ripe, fresh finish at the same time. This is very lovely. Lots of life ahead of it. Just a little unsophisticated.
2005–15

Ramonet

Noël and Jean-Claude
Ramonet
co-proprietors

Domaine Ramonet
4 place des Noyers
21190 Chassagne-Montrachet
Tel: +33 3 80 21 30 88
Fax: +33 3 80 21 35 65
Email: ramonet.domaine@
wanadoo.fr
white: Chardonnay, Aligoté

I sampled the following vintages of Bienvenue-Bâtard-Montrachet in Chassagne in September 2004.

WHITE WINE

BIENVENUE-BATARD-MONTRACHET

Vintage 1999

Subtle nose. Still a little closed. But ripe and concentrated and very distinguished. On the palate a little tight and adolescent. But fullish-bodied. Lots of depth and very good acidity. Great class. Excellent concentrated, honeyed fruit. A firm wine. This is still very young. Potentially very lovely though.

2009–20

Vintage 1998

The colour is quite a lot more developed than the 1999, as is the nose. Ripe, plump, fruit-salady, and fresh if without having that much grip. Less developed on the palate but just about ready. Slightly herbal on the follow-through. Stylish. Good depth. But very good rather than fine.

2005–10

Vintage 1996

Some development on the colour. Lovely nose. Ripe, honeysuckle flavoured, ample, and generous without a hint of high acidity. This means that on the palate we have a wine of real concentration and vigour. Full body. Multi-dimensional and still very youthful. Excellent. Will still improve.

2006–20

Vintage 1995

Youthful colour. Full, rich, concentrated, very high-quality nose. Very impressive. Nutty. Lots of dimension. Full-bodied, very vigorous, very profound and multi-dimensional. Very good grip. Still very young. This is a brilliant example. Marvellous depth of fruit. Really quite powerful. Very, very long. Better even than the 1996 and 1999.

2006–20+

Vintage 1992

Evolved colour. Fresh, fragrant, floral nose. Still with good vigour. Lots of depth and interest. Medium-full body. Good grip. Succulent peachy-hazelnut and peach-stone flavours. Good vigour. *A point.* This is ripe and stylish and generous. Long on the palate and very lovely.

2005–15

Vintage 1990

Fully developed colour. More than the 1992. The nose is fully developed too. We have secondary and tertiary flavours here as well as a touch of oxidation as it developed. Fullish, quite fresh, but a wine for those who like old burgundy. Lovely fruit in a slightly austere way underneath these fully developed aspects. Honeyed, ample flavours. Very good grip. Very good indeed.

2005–08

Vintage 1989

Slightly fresher on the colour than the 1990. Lovely fragrant nose. Soft; echoes of raspberry, but peaches and spring flowers too. Medium-full body. Very lovely on the palate. Less fully developed than the 1990. Better grip. Ripe and fresh and composed. Long and complex and classy. Very fine.

2005–15

Vintage 1988

Youthful colour. Fresh nose. Ample, spicy. The wine is equally plump and vigorous on the palate if with no great depth or concentration. Flowery rather than fruity. Not a blockbuster but holding up well. Very good for what it is but not great. The sample was slightly corked.

drink soon

Vintage 1986

Well-matured colour. Ample nose. Rich and fat. Sensual. Fully mature but with no oxidation. Ripe, rich, and voluptuous. Excellent balance. Fullish-bodied, complex, and with lots and lots of depth. Holding up well. Lots of class. Excellent.

2005–10

Vintage 1983

The last vintage made by grandfather Ramonet. Surprisingly fresh colour, even more youthful than the 1982. The nose is also very crisp. Ripe, rich, and fat, but very fresh. Full but not a hint of the diffuse, the attenuated, or oxidized. Very, very rich and honeyed on the palate. But excellent grip. Not a bit heavy. A wine for food. Very fine.

2005–10

Raveneau

Jean-Marie and Bernard
Raveneau
co-proprietors

9 rue de Chichée
89800 Chablis
Tel: +33 3 86 42 17 46
Fax: +33 3 86 42 45 55
white: Chardonnay

I tasted the following vintages of Raveneau Chablis Montée de Tonnerre in Chablis in February 2004.

WHITE WINE

CHABLIS, MONTEE DE TONNERRE, Vintage 2001

The Raveneaus prefer this to 2000. Just a touch of botrytis. But good fruit and depth and concentration. A ripe, crisp, quite floral wine. Not exactly steely though. Ample and generous already. Unexpectedly good for the vintage but it lacks a little class and Chablis typicity.

2005–09

Vintage 2000

Lighter on the nose than the 2000, but more mineral, more classic. Not a great deal of weight. But it has good length and style. Ripe and fruity. Clean and crisp. Very good but it lacks real depth.

2005–10+

Vintage 1999

Complex nose. Rich and quite fat. Herbal. Lots of depth and class here. Fullish body. Very good fruit. Elegant and profound. Fine and very classy, with just a touch of honey evident at the end.

2005–12+

Vintage 1998

Delicious, pure nose. This is racy and profound. Rich but minerally dry. Energetic. Slight touch of the oak apparent. Quite austere. Long and vigorous. Excellent. *A point.*

2005–12+

Vintage 1997

The colour is beginning to evolve. They preferred to pick early and chaptalize a little bit than delay and risk the fruit turning. Herbal nose. Medium body. This needs drinking quite soon. It lacks a bit of grip and depth. Still decently fresh and stylish. But good rather than fine.

2005–08

Vintage 1996

Mature colour. A wine high in both alcohol and acidity. The vintage seemed very promising, and is still very youthful. But it has never achieved the expectations at the beginning. Full-bodied and quite rich. The acidity is a little marked. The wine isn't very well balanced. Very good but not great.

2005–10

Vintage 1995

Delicious nose. Very smooth, complex, flowery, and spicy nose with a touch of buttered toast. Yet very racy and mineral. Ful-bodied and ample. Very harmonious. Very vigorous. Very long and classy and complex. Very fine. Still very fresh.

2005–12+

Vintage 1991

Complex, mature nose. Quite full. A little attenuated now. Not very stylish but good grip. A wine for food. The finish is rich and complex. Very good but not great.

2005–08

Vintage 1990

More open on the nose than the 1991. More evolved too. Better on aeration. Quite high alcohol but good acidity. Rich, ripe, complex nose. Even better on the palate. Lovely fruit. Concentrated and multi-dimensional. Fresher on the nose. Mature but very youthful still. Very good grip. Long and very lovely.

2005–10+

Vintage 1989

This is indisputably great. Lovely nose. Great presence. Silky-smooth combination of subtle fruit and spices. Aromatic, harmonious, and complex. Extraordinarily fresh for a wine almost 15 years old. Everything totally composed and in place from A to Z. Very long. Very, very classy. Very, very fine indeed. The complete Chablis. You could keep this 30 years.

2005–20+

Vintage 1986

Not by any means an old colour. It seems to have more new wood than recent times. Fullish, very fresh nose. Very concentrated. Very pure. Rich, steely, and minerally yet fat and ample. This is really splendid. Great class. Very, very long. Quite lovely. Still bags of life.

2005–12+

Domaine de la Romanée-Conti

Aubert de Villaine
co-director

Domaine de la Romanée-Conti
21700 Vosne-Romanée
Tel: +33 3 80 62 48 80
Fax: +33 3 80 61 05 72
red: Pinot Noir

I sampled the following magnificent series of wines in Connecticut in March 2003. A huge thank you to Bob Feinn of Mount Carmel Wines & Spirits for having assembled them.

RED WINE

LA TACHE VINTAGE 1995

Good fullish colour. Not a bit too tannic on the nose. Ripe, firm, and succulent. Very good depth. Lovely fruit. Fullish body on the palate. Some tannin but the tannins are ripe and well covered. Very good grip. Indeed quite austere at present. Lots of style and dimension. Real vigour and power. Profound and potentially lovely. Very fine.
2006–26

Vintage 1993

Fine, full colour. Very profound, very classy nose. Excellent fruit. Real concentration. Full body. Rather richer and fatter than the 1995. The tannins are riper and the wine is more succulent. Delicious, multi-dimensional fruit and character. Excellent harmony. This is very fine indeed.
2006–30

Vintage 1992

Fullish, mature colour. Aromatic, fat, quite developed nose. Decent substance and decent freshness on the palate. No lack of depth and interest. Medium-full body. Ample, even rich. Good acidity. Most enjoyable. Ripe and *à point* now. Very good.
2005–10

Vintage 1991

Fullish colour. Now just about ready. Lovely fruit on the nose. Fresh. Not a bit aggressive. Lots of depth. Very stylish. Medium-full weight. Good tannins, now softened. Very fresh, very elegant, very long and harmonious. Lovely finish. *A point* now but will last very well.
2005–15

Vintage 1990

Full colour. Rich and immature. The nose is full and firm. Still closed. But rich and profound. A bit dumb at the start. Full body. Vigorous, even powerful on the follow-through. Splendidly rich fruit. More opulent than the 1993. More volume but less classic. This is a big wine. There is still unresolved tannin here. Strangely it is more oaky than the rest of these younger wines. I prefer the 1993 as it has more class and balance but this is rich, opulent, exotic – still a way from its peak. Very fine plus.
2006–30

Vintage 1988

Medium-full, mature colour. Developed, aromatic nose. A slightly lean touch behind it. Medium to medium-full body. Ripe and fresh. Attractive. Nicely complex. *A point*. No hard edges. Not brilliant but elegant and positive. Long. Less weight but more length and style than the 1991. Fine.
2005–15

Vintage 1985

Medium to medium-full, well-matured colour. Medium-full weight. Complex and very seductive on the nose. Fullish body on the palate despite the colour. Intense, balanced, classy, and refined. Very lovely fruit. Essentially a gentle wine. Very fine plus.
2005–15+

Vintage 1983

Fullish, mature colour. Fullish nose. Aromatic, rich, exotic, concentrated, and complex. Splendidly intense. Very lovely. Very seductive. Full-bodied. Clean and pure. Quite a big wine, almost as big as the 1990. Much bigger than the 1985. Exotic and lovely. Not a bit astringent or over-balanced. Long and multi-dimensional. A really splendid example, if not really very elegant. Very fine.
2005–22+

Vintage 1980

Medium-full colour. Fully mature. Lovely fragrant nose. Rich and mellow. No lack of substance. Medium-full body. Good acidity. But sweet and aromatic. Vigorous, even intense. This is balanced and classy and long on the palate. Fine.
2005–12+

Vintage 1978

Fullish colour. Well matured. More colour than the 1976. Full, rich, vigorous, aromatic, complex, and fat and very ripe indeed on the nose. Full-bodied. Creamy-rich. This is very, very vigorous. Excellent grip. Multi-dimensional. Really profound and very, very lovely. Very fine plus.
2005–20+

CHAMPAGNE

Krug

Rémi Krug
co-director

Champagne Krug
5 rue Coquebert
511000 Reims
Tel: +33 3 26 84 44 20
Fax: +33 3 26 84 44 49
Email: krug@krug.fr
www.krug.com
red: Pinot Noir, Pinot Meunier
white: Chardonnay

I sampled the following vintages of Krug in March 2004. The vintages prior to 1982 are part of the Krug Collection, the series of older wines taken from the Krug reserves.

KRUG

Vintage 1990
Just about to be released. Medium gold colour. Quite developed. This is quite a big, vigorous example. Still youthful. Some structure. Very lovely red fruit flavours. Good grip. Got better mannered in the glass. A little like a cross between 1989 and 1988 but much more youthful at present. Keep for five years at least. Very fine.
2008–40

Vintage 1989
Quite a deep colour. Rich nose. Biscuity. Splendidly opulent. Full-bodied. Very well balanced. Very ripe. This is harmonious, lush, long, and very lovely. A total contrast to the 1988. Very fine.
2005–25

Vintage 1988
Light colour. Flowery nose. Very poised and stylish. Younger than the 1989 (which is why it was put on the market later). Completely different from the 1989. Slightly leaner. More marked acidity. But great depth and class. Splendid purity. Only just ready. Indeed will still improve. Potentially a great wine.
2005–30+

Vintage 1985
Light colour. Like the 1988 there is a reserve about this and the nose is flowery in style. It's a lighter wine, but it is very subtle. I would think there is a little more Chardonnay in the blend here. Medium-full body. A little austerity. Fine but it doesn't have the depth of the 1988. Fully ready.
2005–19

Vintage 1982
Not particularly rich in colour (indeed the 1989 is deeper). The nose is rich but splendidly fresh and complex and profound. A wine which is now completely at its peak. Very lovely fruit. Red berries and peaches. Full-bodied. Lots and lots of depth and dimension. Very long on the palate. Very fine.
2005–20

Vintage 1979
Fully evolved in colour and on the nose. Not old, but with all the extra dimensions of a fully mature wine. Flowery and fruity and exotic wood flavours on the nose. Very ripe. Very seductive. Marvellously fresh. A real classic. Very lovely complex follow-through and finish. Quite delicious.
2005–14+

Vintage 1973
Slightly deeper colour than the 1979. Slightly less complex and more herbal on the nose but the same splendid ripeness on the palate. Very lovely fruit. Very white peaches. Slightly lighter in body. Less fat and complex than the 1979. Less concentration and dimension. Not quite as lovely but quite delicious all the same.
2005–10

Vintage 1966
Rich, full, fully mature colour. A larger than life wine. Big, opulent, even powerful. Mushrooms, cooked fruit, very ripe plums on the nose. On the palate, full-bodied, with hints of mocha. Very, very ripe again. A big wine. Really quite structured. Splendid but a wine for food.
2005–14+

Vintage 1961
Another rich, full, fully mature colour. On the nose this is smooth and aristocratic. Great complexity and finesse. Fullish-bodied. Great dimension. Marvellous balance. Really very fine indeed. Much more subtle than the 1966. A great wine.
2005–20+

Vintage 1959
Rich, full colour. Fully evolved. Rich, ripe, succulent, and opulent on the nose. Splendidly fruity on the palate. A real fruit salad. Full-bodied and very, very rich. Very, very seductive. Almost sweet. Yet the finish is complex, very fresh and very long. Quite delicious. Very lovely indeed.
2005–10+

Vintage 1949
Slightly light in colour. Very, very lovely, complex, elegant nose. A very subtle wine. Slightly lacking in fruity splendour. The ripeness has dried up a little. Still harmonious and classy. But drink soon. Very, very fine.
drink soon

Pol Roger

Hubert de Billy, Patrice
Noyelle, and Christian
Pol Roger
*the three members of the
Directoire*

Champagne Pol Roger
1 rue Henri Lelarge
51206 Epernay
Tel: +33 3 26 59 58 00
Fax: +33 3 26 55 25 70
Email: polroger@polroger.fr
www.polroger.co.uk
red: Pinot Noir, Pinot Meunier
white: Chardonnay

The following wines were sampled in Epernay in February 2004.

BRUT

Vintage 1996
Fine, firm, crisp, minerally nose. Lots of depth and concentration. Still very youthful. Full body. Splendid ripe, concentrated, peachy fruit. Very good grip. This is a very lovely, multi-dimensional wine. It will still improve. Very long and complex. Very elegant. Very fine – perhaps very fine indeed in three to four years' time.
2008–25+

Vintage 1995
A touch floral-herbal on the nose. Rather more developed but less depth and concentration than the 1996. Medium-full weight. Ripe and harmonious and long and classy. Just about ready. Fine.
2005–20

Vintage 1993
Fresh, flowery, fully mature nose. But high-toned and supple. Medium to medium-full weight. Good acidity. But a relatively light, uncomplicated wine in this company. Yet a wine with a lot of charm. Very good plus.
2005–10

Vintage 1990
Very lovely nose. Rich, now with some of the secondary flavours of a fully mature wine. Biscuity and buttery, even slightly mushroom-y. Full body. Lots of depth here. A brilliant example. Now *à point*. Lots of dimension. Very fine balance. Complex. Very fine indeed.
2005–20+

Vintage 1989
Very lush and ripe on the nose. Fat and seductive. Medium-full body. Fruit-salady in flavour. Not a bit like the 1990. None of the digestive biscuit and gingerbread of that vintage. But rich and complex and well balanced. Fine. *A point* now.
now–2015

Vintage 1988
Cool, youthful, and very subtle on the nose. This is very lovely indeed. Fullish body. Very good grip. Still very fresh. It seems younger than the 1990 and 1989. Very complex. Very, very long on the palate. Very, very elegant. In its own way as lovely as the 1990. Very fine indeed.
2005–20+

CUVEE SIR WINSTON CHURCHILL

Vintage 1995
Splendid nose. Very fresh. Very distinguished. Very profound. Still very youthful. Fullish body. Splendid vigour and balance. Very pure. Quite austere still. Very, very lovely cool fruit. Lovely long, discreet finish. Very fine indeed. Will still improve.
2006–26+

Vintage 1993
Lovely nose. Discreet and flowery. Very elegant and subtle. A little lighter than the 1995. Medium-full body. Ripe and stylish and very appealing. Not as serious as the 1995 but very lovely. Very classy. *A point* now.
2005–16

Vintage 1990
Rich, fat nose. Like the Vintage 1990, some biscuit and other mature Champagne flavours on the nose. This is very, very fine wine. Full-bodied, splendidly fresh and pure on the palate. Very concentrated. Excellent grip. Very youthful still. Very complex at the end. Much younger on the palate than the nose. Brilliant! Only just ready.
2005–26+

Vintage 1988
Discreet nose. More youthful than the 1990. Yet some toasted touches as it evolved. Very complex and discreet. Not as flamboyant as the 1990. More subtle. This is quite superb on the palate. Touches of nougat glacé. Very long and multi-dimensional. Even better than the 1990. The finish is splendid. Utterly marvellous. A great wine from start to finish.
2005–26+

BRUT CHARDONNAY

Vintage 1988
Crisp, fresh, very elegant nose. This is a distinguished wine. Very subtle. A lot of depth and dimension here. Very, very high-class fruit. Fullish body. Splendidly balanced. Easily the best of the 1996, '95, '93, '90, and '88 series of Brut Chardonnay. Very long, very lovely. Very fine.
2005–20

Louis Roederer

Jean-Claude Rouzaud
managing director

Champagne Louis Roederer
21 Boulevard Lundy
51053 Reims
Tel: +33 3 26 40 42 11
Fax: +33 3 26 47 66 51
Email: com@champagne-
roederer.com
www.champagne-
roederer.com
red: Pinot Noir, Pinot Meunier
white: Chardonnay

I sampled the following wines on a visit to Roederer in September 2001.

ROEDERER BRUT VINTAGE
Vintage 1995
Magnum. A little Chardonnay, not so high-quality
Pinot Noir. Ripe. Still very youthful. Marked Pinot Noir
flavours. Very lovely fragrant fruit. A bit too young really
but high quality and splendidly balanced. Very long and
very complex. Very classy. Fine.
   2005–20

CRISTAL
Vintage 1995
Magnum. There is a marked difference in refinement
and definition. Rich, clear-cut, clean, and flowery.
Higher toned than the Brut Vintage. Slightly more
marked acidity. Very long and subtle. Very lovely.
   2005–20

Vintage 1993
Bottle. Leaner on the nose than the 1995. Slightly
less ripe fruit. More vegetal/herbal than the 1995.
On the palate this is crisp and stylish. But it doesn't
have the depth and definition of the 1995. Very good.
   2005–09

ROEDERER BRUT VINTAGE
Vintage 1990
Magnum. Full, rich, and meaty. A lovely nose with
a touch of digestive biscuit. Lots of very creamy-rich
fruit. This is better than most of the vintages of Cristal.
Still very young. Bags of life. Very fine.
   2005–12

CRISTAL
Vintage 1990
Magnum. Fat, rich, nutty, spicy, and voluptuous on the
nose with just a suggestion of reduction. Quite sizeable.
Marvellous ripe, complex fruit on the palate. This is very
lovely. Peaches, raspberry, and cream. Long and subtle.
Very fine indeed.
   2005–15

Vintage 1989
Magnum. This is very refined. More depth and class
even than the 1990. Quite remarkable. On the palate
more vinosity and intensity. Rather younger than the

1990. Will still improve. Lots and lots of character.
But it must be drunk with food. Excellent.
   2005–20

Vintage 1988
Magnum. Marvellously restrained, delicate, flowery
nose. It seems to have more acidity and even more
Chardonnay. Complex, fresh, and feminine. Not nearly
as rich or as fruity as the 1989 and 1990 but very stylish.
Less dimension but good intensity at the end. Fine.
   2005–08

Vintage 1985
Magnum. Excellent balance and definition. Very crisp
and concentrated. Lots of depth. Fullish body on the
palate. *A point* now. Rich. Not as fine at the end as
1989 or 1990. Not the same dimension but very fine.
   drink quite soon

Vintage 1983 (A)
Disgorged at usual time. Magnum. Plump, pleasant nose.
Good freshness. Medium-full body. Fully matured on the
palate. A touch sweet-sour at the end, with a little cooked
apples. It lacks a little elegance. Very good at best.
   drink soon

Vintage 1983 (B)
Disgorged three days ago. Magnum. Certainly seems
to have more depth and freshness than the above,
but not as much difference as eight years more before
disgorgement would suggest. A little yeastier. Slightly
heavy. Again it lacks a bit of flair. Very good at best.
   drink soon

Vintage 1982
Full, fat, rich, and meaty. Another wine for food.
Vigorous, succulent, and profound. Lots of depth.
Lots of substance. Lovely finish. Very fine indeed.
   2005–10

Vintage 1979
Magnum. Surprisingly elegant on the nose. Complex,
flowery fruit. One of the best of the series. Lovely fruit:
ripe peaches, raspberries, and cream again plus good
acidity. Less spice than 1990 (less heat prior to harvest),
but more style. Excellent. Will keep well. *A point.*
   2005–10

ALSACE

Trimbach

The Trimbach family

Maison Trimbach
15 route de Bergheim
68150 Ribeauvillé
Tel: +33 3 89 73 60 30
Fax: +33 3 89 73 89 04
Email: contact@maison-trimbach.fr
www.maison-trimbach.fr
white: Riesling

The following wines were sampled in Ribeauvillé in June 2004.

WHITE WINE

CLOS SAINTE-HUNE

Vintage 2003
The nose is still hidden. On the palate the wine is ripe, with a touch of lanolin and cooked apples. Medium to medium-full body and concentration. Decent but only adequate acidity. It lacks the minerally steeliness and the dimension it usually has.
2010–20

Vintage 2002
Marvellous nose. Splendidly pure and racy. Still very young. Full body. Very concentrated, intense, and very lovely fruit. This has great energy. The follow-through is rich but bone dry and very complex and classy. Potentially a great bottle. All the splendid austerity of this great *climat*.
2015–40

Vintage 2001
Lovely nose. Pure and classy and rather more accessible than the 2002. But a very fine expression of Riesling fruit. Not as massively concentrated as the 2002 on the palate. But splendidly balanced. Very ripe. Full body and ample and very, very elegant. Lovely complex, classy follow-through. This is potentially great too. Very complete. A real classic.
2012–35

Vintage 2000
Deeper colour than the 2001. This is ripe, even lush for Clos Sainte-Hune. Full-bodied and fat. Rather more evolved. Dry but less refined, less steely than the 2001. Higher in alcohol. Just slightly clumsy at present. Slightly adolescent. Very good but not great.
2009–20+

Vintage 1999
Lovely nose. Not as clumsy as the 2000. Some evolution. On the palate this is ripe and generous and balanced, but it doesn't have the grip and depth of the 2001. Better class and balance than the 2000, but less energy than 2001. Fine.
2009–25

Vintage 1998
Very classic nose. Now a little evolved. Lovely fruit. Concentrated and austere. Very good acidity. Ripe and vigorous. Long and lovely. A little more weight and grip. Some of the fruit was attacked by noble rot. Fine too, but perhaps the 1999 has more class.
2008–25

Vintage 1997
Open, quite evolved nose. Lots of lovely, very ripe fruit. Easy to appreciate. Quite concentrated. Decent acidity. But not as long or as classy as the 1998. Very good plus.
2006–16

Vintage 1996
Splendid nose. Great class and distinction here. This is pure and mineral. Quite high in acidity (5.9). Very fresh and clean. Underneath splendid concentration and austerity. Fullish body. Vigorous, concentrated, and very lovely. Very long. Very fine plus.
2009–35

Vintage 1990
Quite an evolved colour. Very, very lovely nose. Fragrant, complex, pure, elegant, and very, very fine quality. Quite brilliant on the palate. Now ready. This is well nigh perfect. All the elements splendidly in place. Very, very long.
2005–20

Vintage 1971
Quite an evolved colour and nose. This is fuller and fatter than last time out but equally refined. Very lovely fruit. Getting gently towards the end. Still fresh. Still lovely.
drink soon

Florent Baumard

Florent Baumard
proprietor

Le Domaine des Baumard
La Giraudière
49190 Rochefort sur Loire
Tel: +33 2 41 78 70 03
Fax: +33 2 41 78 83 82
Email: info@baumard.fr
www.baumard.fr
white: Chenin Blanc

I sampled the following wines at Rochefort in February 2003.

DRY WHITE WINE

SAVENNIERES, CLOS DU PAPILLON

Vintage 2000
Lighter colour than the above. Cleaner, more positive nose. Leaner but better grip. More definition. Better complexity and elegance in the fruit. Balanced and long. Very good indeed.
2005–15

Vintage 1999
Quite ripe on both nose and palate. Even a hint of sweetness here. Fullish body. Rich. Slightly heavy. This is not my style, being a little overripe. But it has grip and length.
2005–11

Vintage 1998
Quite different to the above. Much less heavy and four-square on the nose. High-toned, fragrant, and sherbet-lemony. Medium body. Fresh. Decent fruit. It tails off a bit at the end but quite good. Ready.
2005–09

Vintage 1997
The nose is a little closed-in and doesn't show as well as the above. This is drier on the palate and though it has good grip, it hasn't as ample fruit. Very good but I prefer the above. A bad bottle? This is a fine vintage.
2005–13

Vintage 1990
This is a bit pinched on the nose and has a touch of sulphur. Some richness underneath and it has the grip to support it. Is this adolescence? Will it ever come round?
2005–09

Vintage 1989
Very interesting, individual nose. Both grilled and herbal flavours. Clean and quite a lot drier than the above. Full-bodied, rich, balanced, and stylish. Much better than the Clos du Papillon 1990. Very curious. This is long and finely balanced. Complex. Very good indeed.
2005–09

SWEET WHITE WINE

QUARTS DE CHAUME

Vintage 2001
Full but quite dry nose. Splendidly concentrated. Very good acidity. Very honeyed. This seems fatter and with more botrytis than the 2000. Very good grip underneath. Medium to medium-full weight. It improved greatly in the glass. Long. Fine.
2008–38

Vintage 2000
Medium to medium-full weight. Not as rich as the 2001, I think, but it has very good grip and it is long and stylish. Lovely fruit. Still very fresh. This is complex and elegant and very good indeed.
2006–30

Vintage 1990
Youthful colour. Quite dry on the nose. Very good fruit. Gently sweet. Fresh and elegant, and even delicate on the palate. Much drier than I had expected. But rich and concentrated and much more elegant and harmonious. Long and very classy. Lovely. Vigorous and energetic. Lots of life ahead of it. Very fine.
2005–13+

Vintage 1989
Youthful colour. Just a little fatter and richer on the nose than the 1990 but quite dry nevertheless. Still quite sweet. This is very lovely indeed. Marvellously complex, profound fruit. Splendid balance. Very, very long and elegant and poised. Super. Really impressive. Splendidly vigorous still. It will last for ages. Very fine indeed.
2005–18+

Vintage 1976
Mid-gold colour. Old and honeyed, and, for the first time, oaky. This oak is quite rigid. Good grip. Despite the colour it seems fresh and quite youthful on the palate. Sweet but perhaps not a lot of botrytis. Long and fat at the end though. Very good indeed.
2005–09

Clos Rougeard

Nady Foucault
co-proprietor

Clos Rougeard
15 rue de l'Eglise
49400 Chac
Tel: +33 2 41 52 92 65
Fax: +33 2 41 52 98 34
red: Cabernet Franc

I sampled the following wines at Clos Rougeard in February 2003.

RED WINES

SAUMUR-CHAMPIGNY
Vintage 2002
This is the basic *cuvée*. The malolactic fermentation is just about finished. A little gas. Medium body. Slightly raw at present but very stylish fruit. Slightly austere. Long and stylish. Very good.
2008–20

SAUMUR-CHAMPIGNY, LE BOURG
Vintage 2002
This is made only in the best years. Still very youthful. Rich and full-bodied. Not too oaky. Lots of lovely ripe fruit. Profound and stylish. Fine.
2009–25

SAUMUR-CHAMPIGNY, LES POYEUX
Vintage 2001
Good colour. Slightly reduced on the nose. But a fat, rich wine. Good grip. This is fullish-bodied, balanced, and succulent. Very harmonious. Very long. Very good indeed.
2007–17

SAUMUR-CHAMPIGNY, LE BOURG
Vintage 2001
Full-bodied, rich, and oaky. Even better acidity. Rather less developed. Finely poised. Very lovely balance. Still very young. Fine.
2009–20

Vintage 2000
Less marked by the oak. Medium-full and very elegant on the nose. Quite lovely. Very good creamy-rich texture. There is something here which reminds me in its own way of Château Margaux. Not a blockbuster but very fine.
2006–17

SAUMUR-CHAMPIGNY, LES POYEUX
Vintage 1999
No Bourg in 1999 and in 1998. Medium weight. Ample fruit. No great depth or concentration but it is fresh and positive all the way through. Well balanced. No hint of diminution at the end. Just about ready. Really very good.
2005–07

Vintage 1997
Fullish colour. Quite a lot of reduction on the nose. Full-bodied, rich, fat, and meaty on the palate. Very ripe tannins. Lovely fresh acidity. This is a potentially very seductive wine. No hard edges. Very ripe. Very long. Very velvety already. Very fine.
2005–18

SAUMUR-CHAMPIGNY, LE BOURG
Vintage 1997
Bottled 30 months after the vintage. Fine colour. Lovely nose. Very, very rich on the nose. Quite masculine on the palate. Higher acidity than in the Poyeux 1997. Slightly more tannin. The new oak is almost absorbed. Very finely balanced. Very classy. It needs time. Very fine indeed.
2007–20+

SAUMUR-CHAMPIGNY, LES POYEUX
Vintage 1993
Good colour. Medium body. No great depth or concentration but balanced, fresh, positive, and with good plump fruit. Good length, if a little one-dimensional. Fine for the vintage though.
2005–07

Vintage 1985
Fullish, mature colour. Ripe and fresh on the nose. Complex and with some of the spices of maturity. Medium-full body. The tannins have now rounded off. But plenty of depth and vigour. Good fresh, positive finish. It will keep well.
2005–10+

Coulée de Serrant

Nicolas Joly
proprietor

Clos de la Coulée de Serrant
Château de la Roche aux
Moines
49170 Savennières
Tel: +33 2 41 72 22 32
Fax: +33 2 41 72 28 68
Email: coulee-de-serrant@
wanadoo.fr
www.coulee-de-serrant.com
white: Chenin Blanc

I sampled the following wines *chez* Joly in April 2003.

WHITE WINES

SAVENNIERES
CLOS DE LA COULEE DE SERRANT
Vintage 2001
"A vintage of light rather than heat," says Nicolas Joly. More concentrated and more depth than the Clos de la Bergerie. Richer and fatter. Even more individuality and class. Almost a suggestion of honey yet bone-dry. Lovely finish. This is very good indeed.
2006–17

Vintage 2000
Rich, complex, bone-dry nose. Not too austere. Fullish-bodied, ripe, round, and full of fruit. This is bursting with flavour. Very impressive. Vigorous, powerful, and delicious. Very lovely balance. Long and multi-dimensional. It could be drunk now but it will be even better in three years' time. Very fine.
2006–20

Vintage 1999
Again a splendid rich, ripe nose. Slightly less concentrated, less grip, and more evolved than the 2000. There is a suspicion of residual sugar at the end. Plenty of fruit. Good acidity. Ample. *A point*. Fine.
2005–15

Vintage 1997
Individual nose. Slightly more residual sugar here (5 g), so a sweet-sour hint to go with the Victoria plums. This is now ready. It has a slightly white-northern-Rhône adolescent touch. Fullish body. Plenty of energy and very good length. Very good indeed.
2005–09

Vintage 1996
A drier, more concentrated, nutty nose. No adolescence here. This is rich, minerally, and profound. Lots of depth and dimension. Very lovely fruit. Quite dry yet not too austere. Very, very long. Very fine.
2005–15

Vintage 1995
Refined, quite dry, flowery nose. This is feminine where the 1996 is masculine. A touch more residual sugar (3 g) than the above. Very lovely fruit-salady fruit. Medium-full body. Intense and long. Lovely. Fine.
2005–12

CLOS DE LA COULEE DE SERRANT, MOELLEUX
Vintage 1995
14.8° alcohol and 28 g/l sugar. Slightly adolescent nose. Fullish body. Very pure. Very good grip. This is not so much sweet as very, very ripe and generous. Lots of energy. It needs time. Fine.
2005–35

CLOS DE LA COULEE DE SERRANT
Vintage 1994
Quite a different nose. There is lemon balm here, mint, and pine needles. A lighter wine than the 1996 and 1995. Good acidity. Slightly less ample and fat. There is a suspicion of astringency on the palate. Ripe and most enjoyable though. Very individual. Drink quite soon.
2005–08

Vintage 1991
Dry and really quite austere on the nose. A little bit too much sulphur here. It still shows. Not a lot of fruit or generosity. Medium-full body. *A point*. Unexciting.
2005–08

Vintage 1990
Just a suggestion of reduction on the nose. Better on the palate. Firm. Quite rich and ripe but a little hard. It lacks generosity. Fullish body. Again a touch of sulphur on the palate. Not brilliant either. "A bit animal," says Nicolas Joly.
2005–10

Vintage 1989
Riper and more supple on the nose than the 1990. But again a bit of a heavy hand with the sulphur. Decent fruit if not much grace or elegance. Slightly pinched at the end. Drink soon.
2005–06

Couly-Dutheil

The Couly family

Domaine Couly-Dutheil
12 rue Diderot
37500 Chinon
Tel: +33 2 47 97 20 20
Fax: +33 2 47 97 20 25
red: Cabernet Franc

I sampled the following wines in Chinon in February 2003.

RED WINES

CHINON, CLOS DE L'ECHO

Vintage 2002
Fine colour. Complex, chocolate-mocha nose. Liquorice and even leather. Full-bodied. Quite tannic but very good ripe tannins. Very good concentrated fruit. Excellent grip. This is going to be very fine.
2012–40

Vintage 2001
Fine colour. Fine nose. Rich and ample. Concentrated and impressive. Lots of depth here. Quite round and un-aggressive yet full-bodied, tannic, and virile. Very good acidity. Long, complex, and classy. Lovely ripe fruit. Very impressive. A lovely seductive wine. Fine.
2009–20

Vintage 2000
Very good colour. Quite a different personality because no micro-oxygenation and a wine with more aggressive tannins than the 2001 anyway. Fullish, ripe, slightly austere, slightly hard nose. Better on the palate. Good grip. No lack of fruit and the tannins are not too tough. Good length. Very good. Maybe even better if it gets more generous as it softens.
2008–18

Vintage 1999
Good colour. Less volume, but rounder, riper, and more sophisticated on the nose than the 2000. This is now more or less *à point*. Medium body. Good plump attack. It lacks a little grip and tails off at the end but not too short. The finish is still fresh. Still stylish. More vigour than most. A very good example of the vintage.
2005–10

Vintage 1998
Medium colour. Quite a developed nose. Plenty of interest and freshness if no great grip, weight, or depth. This is a lovely example of what is, after all, a lesser vintage. Good medium structure. Ripe and fresh. No weakness. Surprisingly elegant and complex.
2005–07

CHINON, CLOS DE L'ECHO, CRESCENDO

Vintage 1997
Fullish colour. Quite an oaky wine on the nose. On the palate only medium body. But very good ripeness and richness. Lush, succulent, and seductive. Good acidity. Good length if not exactly very vigorous or virile. Even stylish and complex. But a little too much oak for my taste. Just about ready.
2005–11

CHINON, CLOS DE L'ECHO

Vintage 1996
Fine, full, backward colour. Round, ripe, full if with slightly reductive tannins on the nose. Full-bodied, rich, and vigorous. Good grip. Fresh and full of interest. I don't think the tannins will ever be other than slightly astringent. Their evolution was obviously blocked by hydric stress. It finishes long though. It will still develop. Very good indeed.
2005–15

Vintage 1990
This is like a more stylish example of the above. The nose similarly just a little unstylish. Slightly less substantial. Slightly better tannins but slightly less grip. Ripe, stylish fruit on the palate. Now *à point*. Very good indeed again.
2005–10

Vintage 1989
Full colour. Rich, abundant nose. Plenty of substance here. Very good structure. Full body and with lovely ripe tannins. There is a certain gaminess about the flavours, but the wine is very impressive if not completely elegant. More of a Cahors than a Chinon. *A point*. Fine.
2005–12+

Vintage 1964
This has always been a great wine: perhaps the best red Loire I have ever had. Here, direct from the Couly cellars it is still magnificent. Full-bodied, remarkably fresh, complex, and above all elegant. Multi-dimensional. Very, very long. Lovely. Quite splendid. If you can, even rarely, produce wine as good as this, it proves that you are from a really serious appellation. Very fine indeed.
2005–14

Didier Dagueneau

Didier Dagueneau
proprietor

Domaine Didier Dagueneau
Bourg
58150 St-Andelain
Tel: +33 3 86 39 15 62
Fax: +33 3 86 39 07 61
white: Sauvignon Blanc

I sampled the following wines in St-Andelain in February 2003.

WHITE WINE

POUILLY-FUME, SILEX

Vintage 2001
Ripe nose. Gently oaky. Fresh and very elegant. Lovely fruit here. Very harmonious. Fullish-bodied and balanced. Intense and vigorous. Still very youthful. Still a little raw. Long and multi-dimensional on the palate. Fine.
2006–12

Vintage 2000
Quite exotic, almost tropical fruit on the nose. Full. Very ripe, yet not too much so. Good grip but not the greatest acidity. Ample. Plenty of drive. Lush. Finishes well. It improved in the glass. Less heavy than it seemed at first. Ripe. Very good style. Fine.
2006–12

Vintage 1999
A little reduction at first. This blew off after a while. Ripe on the nose. Not as exotic as the 2000 nor as pure or as concentrated as the 2001. Medium-full body. Plump and now soft. The acidity level is not very high. But this means that the wine is round and ready for drinking. Not too long or too complex and slightly more vegetal but very good.
2005–08

Vintage 1998
Classic nose. Ripe and fresh. The oak is well integrated into the wine. Medium-full body. Good depth and class and complexity. *A point* but still with plenty of grip at the end. Composed and harmonious. Very classy. Very long. Very fine.
2005–09

Vintage 1997
A little weak on the nose. It lacks a bit of freshness and vigour as well as size. Medium body. Fresher on the palate than on the nose. But quite evolved. At first ripe and attractive if without the dimension of the 1998. Nor the finesse of the fruit. But as it evolved I found it better than the 1999. Fresher too at the end. Very good plus.
2005–07

Vintage 1994
There is some age here, but still plenty of interest. Cool. I think this always lacked a little real richness but it is fresh and balanced, elegant and complex. It would be better with food. Long. Still has a lot to commend it. An elegant if slightly austere example. Very good plus.
drink soon

Vintage 1993
This also has a little age, but the age shows itself in a different, rather more vegetal way. Medium-full body. Ripe, exotic, fat, and voluptuous. Not too herbaceous. Plump and still vigorous. A little more so than the 1994. I find the 1994 more complex and more elegant but this is very good.
drink soon

Vintage 1991
Because of hail the harvest was a mere 8 hl/ha. Dagueneau made one single Pouilly-Fumé *cuvée*. Remarkably fresh and fine on the nose. Crisp, complex, ripe, and classy. Fullish body. Very integrated. Not a bit herbaceous. Lovely. Very fine. It will still keep well.
2005–07

Vintage 1990
This is very lovely indeed: full, mature, composed, harmonious, classy, and profound. Ripe, rich, and concentrated, but with very good grip. Not quite as fresh on the palate as the 1991, but with more depth and class. Much fuller and fatter. Excellent. Still has life.
2005–07

Vintage 1989
The first year Didier Dagueneau used demi-muids (300-litre barrels). Less stylish, more evolved, and much more vegetal, now in a rather crude way. It was full-bodied, rich, and exotic once. Obviously a hot year, but it probably always lacked a bit of freshness.
drink up

Vintage 1988
Less substance than the 1989 but fresher and a lot more interesting. Medium weight. Ripe. Slightly cool. Only medium concentration, but quite crisp. Still stylish. No hurry to drink up. Very good indeed.
2005–07

Philippe Foreau

Philippe Foreau
proprietor

Domaine du Clos Naudin
14 rue de la Croix Buisée
Tel: +33 2 47 52 71 46
Fax: +33 2 47 52 73 81
white: Chenin Blanc

I sampled the following wines in Vouvray in February 2003.

DRY WHITE WINE

VOUVRAY, SEC

Vintage 2000
Made *sec, demi-sec,* and *pétillant*. Good natural alcohol: 13°. Philippe Foreau considers this superior to 1998. Fat and spicy with slightly hot buttered toast on the nose. Vigorous and rich. More depth, energy, complexity, and volume than the 1998. More class. Needs time.
2006–26

Vintage 1998
Still quite closed-in. Full, fat aromas. Lovely plump, plummy nose. Good acidity. Minerally. Quite austere. But now quite soft and fat. This is just about ready. Long and vigorous. Classic and beginning to get complex. Very good indeed. But better in five years.
2005–13+

Vintage 1996
A bit more ripeness than 2000, just at the limit (13.5°) not to be forced into *demi-sec*. Very fine maturity in the fruit. A lovely full-bodied, mineral wine with excellent acidity. More, it seems, raciness than the 1998 and 2000. Splendid fruit. Very fresh. I love this. Peaches rather than plums and mirabelles. Fine. Will still improve.
2005–10+

SEMI-SWEET WHITE WINE

VOUVRAY, DEMI-SEC

Vintage 2002
Very clean, with pure grapes and passion-fruit on the nose. Very fresh. Creamy. Very ripe with very, very good acidity. This I think is going to be like the 1996 *sec*. Exotic aspects. Very lovely and promising. A vintage rescued by a splendid September. It needs ten years.
2012–30

Vintage 1995
Normal, warm climatic conditions, producing a wine of considerable harmony and refinement. Full body. Rich and still very young. A cornucopia of fruit. Minerally underneath and still quite firm, but with a splendid depth, vigour, and grip. Lots and lots of substance here. Splendid. It needs ten years. But can be enjoyed in three.
2008–28

Vintage 1989
Hot vintage conditions. Honeyed, hot butter, slight touch of butterscotch. Full body. Minerally underneath. Yet very rich. This is ripe, fat, and slightly grilled. It finishes very fresh. Yet just a very little hint of heaviness and a touch of built-in sulphur on the finish. Very good.
2005–09

SWEET WHITE WINE

VOUVRAY, MOELLEUX

Vintage 1985
Light golden colour. Very fresh and youthful on the nose. Honey and flowers. Very poised and relaxed. Sweeter on the palate. Fruit salad flavours. Highish acidity. Remarkably clean and uncloying. Medium-full body. Very harmonious. Very long. Very fine. Ready but will last for ages.
2005–15+

Vintage 1976
Golden, almost bronzed colour. Not very rich but fully ready. Quite evolved. Slight burnt caramel, candied peel flavours. Obviously quite a hot year, but it has lost some of its sugar. Sweeter on the palate. Very good acidity. Quite full body, even chunky. Plenty of depth and interest. Now at its best. Very fresh at the end. Fine. Drink soon.
2005–09

VOUVRAY, MOELLEUX RESERVE

Vintage 1997
"Réserve" means *pourriture noble*. Golden colour. Still a bit closed on the nose. Quite a lot of mandarin, lemon, and passion-fruit with high-toned acidity. Medium-full body. Lovely balance. Very stylish. Very racy. Apricots and cream on the palate with a zip of lemon. Long and very clean and intense. Still needs time. Fine.
2009–25+

Vintage 1989
155 g/l of sugar. Rather more botrytis. A richer, more concentrated vintage than 1997. Golden colour. Fat and ripe and abundant. Slightly closed on the nose. White peaches, spices, and gingerbread. Full body on the palate. Rich and concentrated. Excellent balancing acidity. Quite a lot of vigour and power at the end. Will still improve. Very long. Foreau says not at its best until 2023. I think more like 2011. Very youthful. Very fine.
2011–40

Huët

Noël Pinguet
estate manager

L'Echansonne
Domaine Huët
11 rue de la Croix Buisée
37210 Vouvray
Tel: +33 2 47 52 78 87
Fax: +33 2 47 52 66 74
Email: contact@huet-echansonne. com
www.huet-echansonne.com
white: Chenin Blanc

I tasted these wines *chez* Huët in February 2005.

DRY WHITE WINE

VOUVRAY, CLOS DU BOURG, SEC

Vintage 2000
Lovely Victoria plum, greengage-flavoured nose. Fullish body. Rich. Fresh and youthful. Good acidity. Lovely fruit. Ripe and ample. Very long and complex. Just ready. Fine.
2005–16

Vintage 1999
More floral and herbal than the 2000. Slightly *iodé* and the colour is more evolved. Medium-full body. Plump, round and full of fruit. Less minerally and racy. Now *à point*. Not the finesse of 2000 but long and very good.
2005–10

Vintage 1998
Quite dry and austere on the nose. Medium-full body. It lacks the charm of the 1999 and 2000 at present on the attack, but the finish is plumper and fruitier. Better with food. Not as much to it as the 2000 but better than the 1999. It will still improve. Very good indeed.
2005–12

SEMI–SWEET WHITE WINE

VOUVRAY, CLOS DU BOURG, DEMI–SEC

Vintage 2001
Delicate nose. Slightly adolescent. A little SO_2 combined. Only a little sugar, but enough to add a peachy element to the usual Victoria plum/greengage. Medium-full body. Good acidity. Will be very good indeed.
2006–16

Vintage 1995
Ripe, pure, and fullish on nose and palate. A vigorous, ample follow-through. There is concentration and fat here. Still very young. Lovely. Fine. Will last for ages.
2005–13

SWEET WHITE WINES

VOUVRAY, CLOS DU BOURG, MOELLEUX

Vintage 1985
Very fresh colour for a sweet wine of seventeen years of age. Beautiful nose. Marvellous combination of spring flowers and soft fruit. All very high-toned and elegant.

Splendidly mineral. Fullish body. Very youthful still. Not that sweet either. But very, very complex, stylish, and harmonious. Very fine.
2005–20+

Vintage 1971
Bronze colour. Faint touches of caramel and things cooked in bonfires (or roast chestnuts) on the nose. This has matured well. Not that sweet. But fresh and complex. Very good acidity. Ripe and round and long and lovely. Still bags of life. Fine.
2005–10+

VOUVRAY, CLOS DU BOURG, MOELLEUX, PREMIERE TRIE

Vintage 1997
Half-botrytized, half-*passerillé*. Quite a youthful colour. Rich, slightly closed nose. Not adolescent but quite dry. A gently sweet wine, but without a great deal of power or backbone. A delicate, feminine *moelleux*. Nicely fragrant. Good acidity. Long and stylish. Fine.
2007–27

Vintage 1990
More bronzed colour than the 1989. This is more evolved. Only botrytis here, unlike the 1989. Splendidly rich and sweet. Real honey, with acacia flowers in it. Full body. Balanced, silky-smooth and complex. Very youthful but very lovely.
2005–20+

Vintage 1989
Youthful, deep yellow colour. Still very closed-in on the nose. No botrytis, only *passerillage*. Fuller-bodied, firmer, and more youthful than the 1990. It will still evolve. Great energy here. Rich and powerful. Fine.
2008–30

VOUVRAY, LE HAUT LIEU, MOELLEUX

Vintage 1947
Deep colour. Splendidly concentrated. No longer that sweet but marvellously ripe fruit. Very complex. Full-bodied, vigorous, rich, and honeyed. Very good grip. Splendid fruit. Fat, rich, and concentrated.
2005–15+

Charles Joguet

Jacques Genet, François
Delaunay, and Michel Pinard
the Charles Joguet team

La Dioterie
37220 Sazilly
Tel: +33 2 47 58 55 53
Fax: +33 2 47 58 52 22
Email: joguet@
charlesjoguet.com
www.charlesjoguet.com
red: Cabernet Franc

I sampled the following wines in the splendid Marçay *cave* in February 2003.

RED WINES

CHINON, LES VARENNES DU GRAND CLOS

Vintage 2001
Fresh. Medium to medium-full body. Balanced
and stylish. Clean and pure. Quite round and fat
and with good acidity. Long and elegant. Very good.
2005–12

CLOS DU CHENE VERT

Vintage 2001
Fuller colour. Fuller, richer, and more muscular on the
nose. Concentrated and tannic but not in an aggressive
manner. This is a proper *vin de garde*. Plenty of depth.
Very lovely fruit. Good grip. Fine.
2008–20

CLOS DE LA DIOTERIE

Vintage 2001
Firmer and less advanced than the Clos du Chêne Vert.
The tannins are a little more evident, but the wine has
better acidity. This needs time and to be drunk with
food. Very stylish. At present, more depth if not quite
the charm. Very long. Fine plus for a vintage which is
very good.
2010–26

Vintage 2000
Good colour. Full, tannic, rich, and muscular. This has
gone into its shell a little. It seems to have a bit more
substance, certainly more tannin than the 2001, but
perhaps slightly less finesse. Quite spicy. Good grip. Also
very good, but a bit more rough and ready than the 2001.
2009–12

Vintage 1999
Medium colour. Quite velvety on the nose. Round,
elegant, full, and fruity. Quite supple. Medium body. Not a
lot of tannin. Ripe enough. Decent acidity. Soft finish. This
will inevitably get attenuated in a few years, so drink early.
2005–07

Vintage 1998
Medium colour. Some evolution. A difficult year. The
crop started to rot before it was really ripe. Light and
fruity. Surprisingly clean and agreeable. Pleasant.
drink soon

Vintage 1997
Lightish colour. Now mature. Picked on the edge of
overripeness. Less fresh than the 1998. But a little more
depth and substance. The finish is the best part. Round,
ripe, and quite long. Better than the 1998 and perhaps
better than the 1999. Delicate and stylish. Very good.
2005–09

Vintage 1996
Good colour. Still closed on the nose, but beginning to
round off on the palate. Full body. Very good tannins.
Excellent grip. Stylish ripe fruit. Concentrated and
potentially lush but still quite cool and austere at present.
Long. High quality. Vigorous. It will keep well. Fine plus.
2006–26

Vintage 1995
A very heterogeneous vintage due to an extended
flowering. Medium-full colour. Slightly less classy than the
1996 on the nose. This is medium–full-bodied, slightly
aggressive and vegetal after the 1996, but rich and with
plenty of depth. Best on the finish which is now getting
round and succulent. Long. Very good indeed.
2005–18

Vintage 1993
Not a brilliant vintage but a relief after 1991 and 1992.
Medium to medium-full, fresh colour. Ripe nose. No great
depth or grip but pleasantly fruity. Similar on the palate.
Medium body. Slightly unstylish at the end, lacking
freshness. Beginning to get flabby. Drink soon. Not bad.
drink soon

Vintage 1990
Very good colour. Still fresh. The nose shows no hard
edges and plenty of cool, elegant, pure fruit. Medium-
full body. Good tannins. Lovely fruit except just at the
end. It just lacks a little grip. Fine though. Now *à point*.
2005–09

Vintage 1989
Very fine colour. Concentrated and fresh. Richer
and more concentrated on the nose than the 1990.
Fatter too. A great wine. Fullish body. Lots of depth.
A cornucopia of fruit. Very good grip. Very stylish.
Multi-dimensional. Excellent. Very vigorous. Will last
for ages.
2005–20

Beaucastel

Pierre and François Perrin
co-proprietors

Château de Beaucastel
Chemin de Beaucastel
84350 Courthezon
Tel: +33 4 90 70 41 00
Fax: +33 4 90 70 41 19
Email: contact@beaucastelcom
www.beaucastel.com
red: Grenache, Mourvèdre,
Syrah, Vaccarèse, Muscardin,
Terret Noir, Cinsault, Counoise
white: Grenache Blanc,
Clairette, Bourboulenc,
Roussanne, Picpoul, Picardin

I sampled the following wines at Beaucastel in October 2004.

RED WINE

CHATEAUNEUF-DU-PAPE, CHATEAU DE BEAUCASTEL

Vintage 2001
Fine, full colour. Rich, ripe, succulent nose. Not a bit aggressive. Very lovely fruit. Fullish body. Very good grip. This has excellent depth and harmony, and very ripe tannins. Abundant, complex, and very stylish. Very fine.
2010–25+

Vintage 2000
Medium-full colour. Soft, exotically ripe, plump nose. Medium-full weight. Very rich, almost jammy, fruit. Very good fruit. Not as classic as the 2001 but a wine of great charm. Splendidly succulent. Fine.
2007–19

Vintage 1999
Fine, full colour. Quite firm on the nose. Full and rather more black-fruity than the 2000. More grip too. Fullish body. There is a very cool, slightly austere, elegant character here which I like very much. A little tannin. Ripe, long, and profound at the end. Fine plus.
2008–20+

Vintage 1998
Very good, full colour. Accessible nose with a touch of spice. Ripe but quite soft. Medium-full body. Fresher on the palate than on the nose. The tannins now just about resolved. Good grip. Stylish, balanced, and fruity. Just about ready. Very good indeed.
2005–15

Vintage 1997
Medium to medium-full colour. Some evolution. Soft, plump nose. No great depth here. A medium-weight, fully mature wine. Ripe, attractive, and fruity. Nice freshness on the palate. Stylish. Very good.
2005–12

Vintage 1996
Fullish colour. A little evolution. Fresh, rich, fullish nose. Abundant, harmonious, and elegant. Fullish body. Good grip. The tannins are now resolved. This has depth, length, and dimension. Nicely cool, like the 1999. Just about ready. Long on the palate. Fine.
2005–18

Vintage 1995
Full colour. Still very youthful. Ripe but rather closed on the nose. Not too burly though. Slightly roasted fruit flavours. Medium-full body. Slightly astringent on the palate. A slight absence of real succulence. Slightly bitter at the end. Decent fruit and acidity but a lack of style. *A point*. Quite good at best.
2005–10

Vintage 1994
Medium-full colour. Now mature. Not a lot of depth on the nose. Fresh and fruity but a little one-dimensional. A lightish wine but fresh and quite stylish. Easy to drink. I get more enjoyment here than with the 1995. Positive finish. Good.
drink soon

Vintage 1993
Medium-full colour. Now mature. Lightish and slightly attenuated nose. Light to medium body. Slightly astringent. This lacks the freshness of the 1994. Fair.
drink up

Vintage 1992
Fullish colour. Still quite fresh-looking. Succulent, positive, attractively fresh, plump nose. Medium-full body. Good grip. This is fruity and elegant and surprisingly harmonious and long on the palate. *A point*. Very good plus.
2005–14

Vintage 1990
Full, vigorous colour. Rich, concentrated, profound nose. There is a lot of depth and quality here. Full body. Very rich and ripe, fat and succulent. Excellent grip. Vigorous, multi-dimensional, long, and classic. Very impressive. This is a very fine wine indeed. Just about ready.
2005–25+

Vintage 1989
Full, vigorous colour. Fat, luscious, succulent, splendidly ripe nose. Fullish-bodied, almost sweet, rich and abundant on the palate. Good acidity if not the grip of the 1990. A more Grenache-flavoured wine. Not quite as glorious but very fine nonetheless.
2005–20

Jean-Louis Chave

Jean-Louis Chave
proprietor

Domaine Jean-Louis Chave
37 Avenue de St-Joseph
07300 Mauves
Tel: +33 4 75 08 24 63
Fax: +33 4 75 07 14 21
red: Syrah

I sampled the following wines in Mauves in October 2004.

RED WINES

HERMITAGE ROUGE

Vintage 2001
Full, youthful colour. Very lovely pure Syrah fruit on the nose. Ripe, rich, full, and firm on the palate. Still slightly austere, but not solid or sturdy. Intense, profound, and classy. Ripe tannins and good grip. Long and distinguished at the end. Has real finesse. Potentially very fine indeed.
2014–40

Vintage 2000
Full, youthful colour. Riper and more opulent on the nose than the 2001, but less depth, substance, and vigour. Fullish body. Good acidity, but the tannins are a little more astringent. Rich though. Long, and with good depth. Fine.
2012–28

Vintage 1999
Fullish colour. Still youthful. Raspberry and cherry elements on the nose. Nothing aggressive here. Fullish body. Ripe, rich, and opulent, with very good acidity. The tannins are softening. Very good follow-through. Clean, pure, classy, and intense. I prefer this to the 2000. Very fine.
2009–30+

Vintage 1998
Medium-full colour. Still quite youthful. Lovely fruit on the nose with a slight touch of austerity. Yet some evolution now. Fullish body. The tannins softening. Slightly less opulent than the 1999 but long and complex and very classy. Very lovely finish. Delicious. Very fine plus.
2010–35

Vintage 1990
Full colour. Still immature. Magnificent nose. Rich, full, concentrated, very profound and classy. Still vigorously youthful, but it is getting there. Full body. Excellent grip. Very fine tannins. Complex, plentiful, balanced, ripe fruit. Still some tannin, but now softening. Long. Distinguished.
2006–40

Vintage 1988
Fullish colour. Still youthful. Lovely nose. Vigorous, rich, and complex. Very fresh. *A point.* Fullish body. Ripe, classy fruit. Still plenty of energy. Balanced, long, and very fine.
2005–30

HERMITAGE RESERVE, CUVEE DE CATHELIN

Vintage 2000
Splendid full, youthful, intense colour. Full, rich, concentrated, quite powerful but creamy-opulent nose. Very ripe indeed. Full body. Very fresh. Quite tannic but the tannins are very ripe. Good grip. A big but vigorous and very harmonious, profound wine. Excellent.
2015–50

Vintage 1998
Excellent, fresh, full colour. Fabulous fruit on the nose. Intense, pure, harmonious, and very concentrated. This is essence of Syrah. Very full but not a bit too sturdy. Some tannin. Excellent acidity. Long and intense and very, very classy at the end. Even better than the 2000. A really great wine.
2012–45

Vintage 1995
A fine colour, now beginning to develop. Subtle nose. Quite exotic and a lot more classy than the "basic". Very lovely fruit with a touch of spice. Fullish body. Some tannin a little bit sturdy. Good grip. This is fine and still needs to be kept.
2009–29

Vintage 1991
Full colour, now showing some development. Like the 1995, this shows the character of the vintage. Ripe, opulent nose. Not as pure as the 2000 or 1998. Full-bodied and rich on the palate. Slightly astringent. Decent acidity but it lacks a little intensity and grip, and therefore elegance. Very good indeed. Not significantly better than the "basic".
2005–18

Vintage 1990
Full, youthful, vigorous colour. Very fine nose. Pure, rich, balanced, slightly austere, ripe, and fragrant. Still a little immature. Rather more backward than the "ordinary". Full-bodied. Concentrated. Very fine grip. Excellent depth and concentration. Splendid fruit. Still some tannins, but they are very ripe. Very, very long on the palate. A great wine as well as a big one but it still needs some time.
2009–50

Guigal

Marcel and Philippe Guigal
father and son co-proprietors

Château d'Ampuis
69420 Ampuis
Tel: +33 4 74 56 10 22
Fax: +33 4 74 56 18 76
Email: contact@guigal.com
www.guigal.com
red: Syrah
white: Viognier

I sampled the following wines in Ampuis in October 2004.

RED WINE

COTE-ROTIE, LA LANDONNE

Vintage 2001
Fine colour. Splendidly concentrated, rich nose. Lovely balance. Very profound. Very ripe. Fullish body. Lots of depth and dimension. Very good grip. Ripe tannins. Stylish and vigorous. Long and complex at the end. Excellent.
2011–36

Vintage 2000
Fine colour. Rich nose. Rounder and riper than the 2001, but perhaps less depth and concentration. Touches of roast chestnuts. On the palate slightly less body and acidity. Medium-full body. Splendidly ripe and fruity. Good tannins. Unlike the 2001, not the backbone or potential for long ageing, but certainly very delicious. Fine.
2009–28

Vintage 1999
Fine colour. A little more austere than the 2000 on the nose without having the depth and volume of the 2001. But very subtle and lovely nevertheless. Lots of fragrant, classy fruits. Medium-full body. Balanced and intense. Very good grip, lots of finesse, and ripe tannins. Long. Complex. Flavours of old roses and raspberries. Beautifully harmonious. Lovely finish. Very fine.
2009–30

Vintage 1998
Medium-full colour. Quite a high-toned, flowery nose. Medium-full weight. Fresh. Just a little tannin. Fragrant. Good acidity. A bit more austere than the 1999. A little less ripe, less fat, and less complex. Very good indeed.
2007–20

Vintage 1997
Slightly more colour than the 1998. Rich, ripe, spicy nose. The new oak is still apparent. Fat and meaty. Fullish body. Abundant. Still just a little tannin. Good grip. Long and satisfying on the follow-through. Fine plus.
2007–30

Vintage 1995
Medium-full colour. Now mature. Ripe nose. Quite concentrated. Good depth here. Fullish body. Plenty of grip. Plenty of fruit. Balanced. Now softening, but vigorous, long, and complex on the palate. Classy. Just about ready. Fine. "A wine for game," says Marcel Guigal.
2005–25

Vintage 1988
Medium-full colour. Still very fresh. Very lovely, aromatic nose. Principally made up of all sorts of exotic woods. Full-bodied, rich, balanced, complex, and classy. Very ripe. Excellent grip. Still very vigorous. This is quite lovely. Very, very long and complex. Very, very lovely finish. Excellent. Will keep for ages.
2005–25

Vintage 1985
Medium-full colour. No sign of age. Splendid nose. Rich, fat, and opulent. Fully mature now. Medium-full body. Good grip. Round and ripe and seductive on the palate. It is not quite as vigorous, complex, and classy as the 1988, but it is plump, ripe, and disarmingly delicious. A wine of great charm. Very long. Fine plus.
2005–18

Vintage 1983
The biggest, most tannic of all the Landonnes. Fullish, vigorous colour. Still firm on the nose. Yet very rich and concentrated underneath. Not a bit hard or sturdy. Full body. Still some tannin. Very good grip though, and no lack of fruit. Better on the nose than on the palate. A wine for food. I prefer the 1988 and the 1985.
2005–20

Vintage 1979
Medium to medium-full colour. Delicious fragrant, flowery nose. But by no means a blockbuster. Medium body. Ripe, but not delicate. Fully ready. Classy and intense. A feminine Landonne. Long. Harmonious. Surprisingly good. The vines were only five years old at the time.
drink soon

Vintage 1978
Good fresh, fullish colour. Lovely nose. Splendidly classy and concentrated. Great class. Very complex and intense. This is at least as good as the best of the above. Fullish body. Vigorous, harmonious, and very, very long. Splendid. Plenty of life ahead.
2005–20

Paul Jaboulet Aîné

The Jaboulet family

Paul Jaboulet Aîné
Les Jalets
BP46 La Roche-sur-Glun
26600 Tain l'Hermitage
Tel: +33 4 75 84 68 93
Fax: +33 4 75 84 56 14
Email: info@jaboulet.com
www.jaboulet.com
red: Syrah

I sampled the following wines at La Roche–sur–Glun in October 2004.

RED WINE

HERMITAGE LA CHAPELLE

Vintage 2001
Full colour. Firm, rich, roasted spices nose. Lots of exotic wood. Full and meaty. Adolescent at present. Full-bodied, vigorous, rich, and tannic on the palate. Very good grip. Fat. Lots of depth here. At present it is difficult to see the elegance. But the finish is long and abundant. Surely fine plus.
2013–40

Vintage 2000
Medium-full colour. Ripe, succulent, blackcurrant-leaf Syrah nose. Very good grip. Medium-full body. Lovely plump fruit. Excellent balance. Very pure and very lovely. A classic. Very long and complex. Fine.
2010–30

Vintage 1998
Medium-full colour. A little brown at the rim. Some gentle evolution on the nose. Plump, balanced Syrah fruit here. Composed and elegant. Medium-full weight. Just a little tannin. Ripe and soft and laid-back. Quite intense but not aggressive. Subtle and long. Very good indeed. Will come round soon.
2006–20

Vintage 1996
Fullish colour. Only a little evolution. Rich, creamy nose. Lovely ripe old viney fruit. A very relaxed wine. Nothing aggressive here. Full-bodied, fresh, and very harmonious. Excellent grip. The tannins now just about softened. Very long. Very lovely. Will last very, very well. Fine plus.
2007–30

Vintage 1995
Full colour. Still very youthful. Firm, tannic nose. A very full-bodied wine, slightly burly at present. Still some tannin. But plenty of fruit and lots of energy. Very good grip. Lots of substance here. Lovely finish. Rich and multi-dimensional. Fine plus. It needs time. Still very, very young.
2009–30

Vintage 1990
Very full, youthful colour. Marvellous nose. Rich, concentrated, profound, and very distinguished.

Now getting accessible. Full body. Still very vigorous, if not powerful. Intense. Still a bit of tannin. Fine grip. Very concentrated fruit. The complete Hermitage. Very, very long. Still needs three or four years at least. Excellent.
2008–50

Vintage 1989
Fine, vigorous colour. Just about mature. Ripe, aromatic nose. Roast chestnut and exotic wood with rich, creamy fruit underneath. Fullish-bodied, plump and balanced. Just about ready. Succulent and seductive. But fresh and with a fine long finish. Fine.
2005–20+

Vintage 1988
Medium-full, mature colour. Slightly austere on the nose. Very good acidity. Nice pure Syrah fruit. But a slight lack of generosity. Firmer than the 1989. More grip. Fullish body. Very classic. No lack of attraction. Long. *A point.* Fine too, in its own way. But quite different from the 1989.
2005–30

Vintage 1985
Fullish, now mature colour. Interesting, spicy nose. Mocha and caramel. Now fully evolved. Medium-full body. Good plump attack. A little lacking grip at the very end but ripe, plump, and attractive. Fully ready. Very good indeed.
2005–15

Vintage 1978
Fine colour. Still very youthful. Marvellous complex, profound, very fresh nose. Full-bodied. Excellent depth and concentration. Excellent grip. Very vigorous still. Multi-dimensional. This is a great wine. Quite splendid!
2005–30+

Vintage 1966
Fine, full, fully evolved colour. Very lovely, very fragrant, velvety-smooth nose. Lots of very lovely fruit. Still very, very fresh. Medium-full body. Good backbone and intensity. Marvellous class. Splendid harmony. Long, lingering finish. Very lovely.
2005–20

Gauby

Gérard Gauby
proprietor

Domaine Gauby
La Muntada
66600 Calce
Tel: +33 4 68 64 35 19
Fax: +33 4 68 64 41 77
Email: domaine.gauby@
wanadoo.fr
red: Grenache, Carignan,
Syrah, Mourvèdre

I sampled the following wines in Calce in January 2004.

RED WINES

COTES DU ROUSSILLON VILLAGES, VIEILLES VIGNES

Vintage 2002
Very good colour. Closed-in on the nose. Not a
blockbuster but very lovely fruit. Concentrated and rich
and very well balanced on the nose. Vigorous. Very, very
long on the palate. Classy. Profound. Very fine.
2012–30

Vintage 2001
Fine colour. The nose is still a little closed-in, but there
is a lot of substance. Fullish. Tannic. Vigorous. Very
good grip. Bigger than the 2000. More backbone. This
is better. Very long. Lots of potential. Very fine indeed.
2012–35+

Vintage 2000
Fine colour. Splendid concentrated fruit on the nose. Lush,
rich, classy, and harmonious and very profound. Fullish
body. Ripe and sophisticated tannins with good acidity
and length. Vigorous. Very lovely and complex. Very fine.
2010–35

Vintage 1999
Medium-full colour. The nose is less ample than the 1998,
though not without interest, but this is more evolved.
Fullish body. Very lovely purity. Generous, balanced fruit.
Not as big as the 1998 but richer and riper. Fine plus.
2006–25

Vintage 1998
Good colour. Still youthful. Full, fat, rich, and
concentrated on the nose. A full-bodied, succulent,
profound, and concentrated palate. Very lovely rich fruit.
Lots of substance. Still some very sophisticated tannin.
This is fine. Long on the finish. An impressive example.
2008–28

Vintage 1996
Medium-full colour. Slightly less backbone than the 1995.
A point now. Good grip. Nicely stylishly succulent. Finishes
very well. Lots of charm. Very good indeed.
2005–10

Vintage 1995
Good full, vigorous colour. Full nose. Lots of depth. Still
young. Classy fruit. Very good tannins. Finely balanced
with grip, intensity, and dimension. Will keep very well.
In fact I think it will still improve. Very good indeed.
2005–15+

COTES DU ROUSSILLON VILLAGES, MUNTADA

Vintage 2002
Very good colour. Still very youthful on the nose, with
some of the leafy aspects of young Syrah, but very, very
rich, ripe, and concentrated. Very fine grip. Full body. Very
sophisticated tannins. A powerful wine of great potential.
2015–30

Vintage 2001
Impressive colour. Very lovely, pure fruit on the nose.
Lovely cream and velvet as well. Not quite as full as the
2000, but complex and stylish. Very good acidity. Long.
Lovely. Great finesse. Perhaps even better than 2000.
2015–35

Vintage 2000
Very fine, full, immature colour. This is less muscular
than the 1999 and even more sophisticated. Fullish-
bodied rather than full but very, very concentrated.
Poised. Multi-dimensional. "This is the justification
of twenty years' work," says Gérard. Marvellous fruit.
Very, very long. A great wine.
2013–45

Vintage 1999
Very full colour. Rich, but much better mannered than the
1998. More classy. Still very youthful. Intense and ripe. Full-
bodied. Very ripe tannins. Quite powerful, but still young.
Very concentrated. Not ready for drinking. Very fine.
2011–35

Vintage 1998
Fullish colour. Very lovely rich concentration. A big wine.
Some tannin. This will still improve. Very good grip. Lots
of vigour and intensity. Plenty of depth and power. In
retrospect Gérard found this "much too larger than life.
Too much oak and torrefaction. It was a wine that got
very good points at the outset but aged badly. Too
powerful. I changed my approach as a result," he said.
2008–28

La Grange des Pères

Laurent Vaillé (left)
proprietor

Domaine de la Grange des Pères
34150 Aniane
Tel: +33 4 67 57 70 55
Fax: +33 4 67 57 32 04
red: Syrah, Mourvèdre, Cabernet
Sauvignon, Carignan

I sampled the following wines in Aniane in February 2004.

RED WINE

VIN DE PAYS D'HERAULT, LA GRANGE DES PERES

Vintage 2002
Medium weight. Red fruit to the fore. Fresh and supple. Not a lot of backbone. Vaillé says this has a burgundian character. It certainly has a burgundian rather than Midi weight. Ripe. Harmonious.
2008–12

Vintage 2001
Just before bottling. Good colour. Ripe, fragrant nose. By no means a blockbuster. Interesting mixture of *provençal* herbs, red and black fruits. At present not very expressive. On the palate, medium-full body, ripe and fruity. A little tannin and a touch of oak. Complex and well-balanced flavour. Nice and cool and fresh. Elegant too. Lovely. Really remarkably subtle. Long at the end. Fine.
2009–15 +

Vintage 2000
Good colour. This is very lovely. Fragrant nose. Very ripe but very cool. Violets as well as plums and damsons and blackberry. Fullish body. Very good tannins. Not a bit southern. Fresh and complex. Very long. Very fine. A bigger and better wine than the 2001.
2010–25 +

Vintage 1999
Good colour. Less concentrated and less rich and ripe on the nose than the 2000. Rather more charm on the palate. Medium-full body. Soft tannins. Good acidity. A slightly cool, less succulent example than the 2000, but long, complex, and very stylish. The difference between this and the above is like the contrast between 1988 and 1990 bordeaux or burgundy.
2010–25 +

Vintage 1998
Good colour. Slightly less sophisticated on the nose with a touch of reduction, which can be released by decanting. Spicy elements like mocha. Full body. A bit closed. Slightly less grip than the two above. Ripe. Slightly rigid. Just a little clumsy, but not short. The finish is positive, but it lacks elegance. Better as it evolved. Two hours later with the meal it was much better and not at all lacking fat.
2008–16

Vintage 1997
Medium-full colour. Lovely soft nose. Mulberries. This is medium-full-bodied and very well balanced. Fragrant, fresh, and delicious now. Plump, round, balanced, and generous. Lovely. A wine of great charm.
2005–12

Vintage 1996
Full, youthful colour. Quite structured and closed-in on the nose. Full, tannic, and quite solid. Similar on the palate. The tannins are a bit astringent. Good acidity, but I don't think it will ever properly soften up. Good at best. Slightly ungenerous. Drink with food. Keep it and hope.
2006–16

Vintage 1995
Fine full, youthful colour. Very impressive on the nose. Ripe and rich and spicy and balanced. Full on the palate. A little solid, like the above. Just a touch astringent but altogether better. The tannins aren't as classy as they are in today's vintages and the wine needs food. Leave it a year. Ripe and complex at the end. Very long. Lots of depth and dimension. Fine.
2005–20

Vintage 1994
Good colour. Now mature. Decent nose. But it lacks the richness and sophistication of the 1995. Medium-full body. A little clumsy astringency. This is much more obviously a wine of the Midi. Decent acidity. Positive finish. But a lack of real velvet or elegance. Good at best.
2005–10

Vintage 1993
Medium-full, mature colour. This is softer and therefore more supple than the three vintages above. In its way like the 1997. Medium-full body. Round. Not as classy but a wine with plenty of charm. Very good. *A point.*
2005–10

Vintage 1992
Laurent Vaillé's first vintage. Medium-full colour. Slightly rustic on the nose. But no lack of fruit or signs of over-extraction. Medium-full body. Slightly hot and southern. Not very sophisticated, but good, especially for a first effort. Ripe and succulent.
drink soon

Montus

Alain Brumont
proprietor

Château Bouscassé
Maumussan
32400 Laguian
Tel: +33 5 62 69 74 67
Fax: +33 5 62 69 70 46
Email: bruno.commercial@
wanadoo.fr
red: Tannat

I sampled the following wines at Château Bouscassé in September 2004.

RED WINES

MADIRAN, CHATEAU MONTUS, PRESTIGE

Vintage 2002
Good colour. Soft, ripe, gently oaky nose. Medium
weight on the palate. Quite developed. No hard edges.
Fresh and ripe. Long and stylish. Will come forward
quite soon. A charming wine.
2008–15

Vintage 2001
Good colour. Rich, black-fruity nose. Medium-full body.
Rich and oaky. Very good acidity. Very long and very
elegant. Lovely finish. Ripe tannins. Very fine.
2010–30

Vintage 2000
Good colour. Firm, quite tannic nose. Quite a full,
structured wine. The tannins dominate at the moment.
Rich and concentrated. Very good grip. Lots of depth.
It just needs time. Fine. But the 2001 is better.
2012–35

Vintage 1999
Good colour. Ripe, medium-weight nose. Medium body.
Less rich, ripe, and fat than the surrounding vintages.
Less grip too. A wine of less dimension and interest.
Good fruit though. Quite good. Just about ready.
2005–10

Vintage 1998
Good colour. Quite an austere, tannic nose. Medium-
full weight. Good ripe tannins, well supported by good
acidity. Lovely black-fruit flavours. Not as big or as
concentrated as the 2000, but long and very stylish.
Fine.
2009–30

Vintage 1996
Good colour. The nose is now softening up. Aromatic
and spicy if not especially classy. On the palate it lacks a
bit of richness and zip. Medium to medium-full body, but
a little charmless. Quite good at best. Just about ready.
2005–09

Vintage 1995
Very good colour. Rich, full, concentrated nose. This is a
lot better than the 1996. Medium-full body. Very good
fruit. Abundant, ripe, and now softening up. Very good
finish. Very good indeed.
2005–20

Vintage 1992
Mature colour. Pleasant fruit on the nose. Medium
body. No great depth or interest but soft. *A point.*
2005–09

Vintage 1991
Good colour. Surprisingly good nose. No lack of fruit
and interest. Medium weight. A little astringent. Good
fruit and acidity. Positive finish. Better with food.
2005–09

Vintage 1990
Very good colour. Rich, full nose. More old-fashioned than
the wines of today. But not rustic. Full, rich, and opulent
on the palate. Good backbone. Very good grip. Plenty of
structure. Long, ample finish. Just ready. Plenty of future.
2005–30

Vintage 1989
Splendid colour. Very impressive nose. Very rich and
concentrated. Very succulent ripe fruit. Lots of depth. Lots
of finesse. Full body. Chocolatey and rich. Very good grip.
Will keep for ages. Even better than the 1990. Very fine.
2005–35

CHATEAU MONTUS, LA TYRE

Vintage 2001
Fine colour. Splendid nose. Rich and concentrated
and very classy. Quite oaky. Full-bodied and very
concentrated. Very intense. This is essence of Tannat,
but in no way over the top. Very impressive. Needs
time. Excellent.
2013–40

Vintage 2000
Very fine colour. Excellent nose. Very, very rich and
succulent. Very ripe tannins. Oaky, profound, and
crammed with fruit. A big wine but not a bit aggressive.
Very good grip. Very fine. But the 2001 is better still.
2010–30

Tempier

Daniel Ravier and
Jean-Marie Peyraud
manager and co-proprietor

Le Plan du Castellet
83330 Castellet
Tel: +33 4 94 98 70 21
Fax: +33 4 94 90 21 65
Email: info@
domainetempier.com
www.domainetempier.com
red: Mourvèdre, Cinsault,
Grenache, Syrah

I sampled the following wines in Bandol in January 2004.

RED WINES

BANDOL, CUVEE MIGOUA

Vintage 2001

Creamy-rich on the nose. So rich it is almost sweet on the palate. Fullish body. Very good tannins. Excellent grip. Very long and concentrated on the follow-through. It will keep for ages. Great finesse. Very fresh. Very fine indeed.

2010–40

Vintage 2000

Fine colour. Very poised black-cherry and chocolate nose. Fullish body. Lovely fruit. Ripe, complex, discreet, and very harmonious. Excellent grip. Very classy and lovely. Just a touch of astringency at the end, so fine, rather than great.

2008–30

Vintage 1998

Fine colour. Very lovely nose. Quite full, but not aggressive. Very rich. Excellent grip. Quite closed-in but very lovely fruit underneath. On the palate this is already velvety. Yet there is lots of energy here and no lack of volume. Very, very long. Potentially voluptuous. Very fresh. Very complex. Very elegant. Very lovely. Brilliant!

2010–35

Vintage 1993

Still quite an immature colour. But beginning to soften up on the nose. Fullish body. Very fresh. Not as much of a blockbuster as 1990 or more recent years but a wine of concentration, grip, and depth. Vigorous and classy. Lovely fruit. Complex. Very long. Fine plus. Just ready.

2005–15

CUVEE CABASSAOU

Vintage 2000

Very fine colour. This is rich and creamy on the nose. Very lovely fruit. Not as adolescently aggressive as the Tourtine. Very full-bodied. Very old viney in flavour. No lack of tannin but essentially very fresh and well balanced. Heaps of dimension at the end. This is very, very lovely. This will be a sumptuous wine when it is mature. Brilliant!

2013–50

Vintage 1995

Very fine colour. Full, very rich and youthful. This is a much more serious wine than the Migoua or the

Tourtine. Full body. Good vigour. Rich and complete. Lovely elegant fruit. Still youthful. Much more classy. Lots of depth. Fine plus.

2006–26

CUVEE TOURTINE

Vintage 2001

A little firmer than the Migoua but equally rich and succulent on the nose. Fullish body. Rather more closed-in. Good tannins. Very good grip. A little more austere, muscular, and *sauvage* at present but equally long and potentially fine.

2010–40

Vintage 2000

Very fine colour. Like the 2001, much more closed on the nose than the Migoua and bigger, sturdier, and more powerful. More adolescent. Full-bodied, tannic, and youthful. But underneath. Very fine fruit and grip and less astringent, more velvety at the end. Lots and lots of depth. Very fine.

2010–40

Vintage 1999

Good colour. As usual a bit gamey on the nose. But, if not as structured as the 2000, it still has no lack of depth and dimension. Slightly astringent on the attack from the tannins, which are not quite as ripe as in 2000, but long, fresh, complex, and classy at the end. Very good indeed.

2008–20

Vintage 1998

Full colour. Again very ample, like the Migoua. Less gamey than usual but slightly more angular. Certainly more backbone and more unresolved tannin. Very good grip. It needs more time. Does it have the seductive appeal of the Migoua? No. But it is a very fine example nonetheless. Very, very long at the end.

2012–45

Vintage 1993

Medium-full colour. It is beginning to show signs of maturity. Slightly more sinew on the nose than the Migoua. Slightly more "southern". A little fresher, fuller, and firmer. Very good grip. Not too gamey. More vigorous. For once I prefer this to the Migoua. Very fine.

2005–20

Trévallon

Eloi Dürrbach
proprietor

Domaine de Trévallon
Vieux Chemin d'Arles
13103 St-Etienne du Gres
Tel: +33 4 90 49 06 00
Fax: +33 4 90 49 02 17
Email: trevallon@wanadoo.fr
www.trevallon.com
red: Cabernet Sauvignon,
Syrah

I sampled the following wines at Domaine de Trévallon in January 2004.

RED WINE

VIN DE PAYS DES BOUCHES DU RHONE, DOMAINE DE TREVALLON

Vintage 2001
Bottled December 19, 2003. Fine, fullish colour.
A touch of chocolate. Slightly austere. But ripe enough underneath. Full-bodied. Some tannin. Very good grip and concentration. Lots of depth here. More alcoholic and more spicy than the 2000. Fine.
2011–30

Vintage 2000
Concentrated, full colour. Lovely nose. Very rich fruit. Very ripe Syrah. Lots of creaminess. Less austere than the 2001, but then a great deal longer, proportionately, in bottle. Very fine grip. Cool. Classic. Full-bodied. Very good tannins. Very lovely fruit. Very fine.
2010–30

Vintage 1999
Medium-full colour. Some evolution. Softer nose. More red fruity. Medium to medium-full body. Only a little tannin. Good freshness but not the concentration and fat of the 2000. Positive, balanced, and stylish at the end. Elegant. In its own way quite burgundian. Very good plus.
2006–16

Vintage 1998
Slightly more colour than the 1999. Less evolved. More structure, but in a slightly robust sense. This is like a Châteauneuf-du-Pape. Fullish body. On the palate very ripe and juicy. But a touch tough and astringent. A wine for food. Very good plus.
2007–18

Vintage 1996
Quite evolved on the nose. A little overripe without being concentrated. Medium to medium-full body. Sufficient acidity, but a little cooked. It lacks a bit of elegance. Fuller than the 1997 but not as stylish.
drink soon

Vintage 1995
Fine, full colour. Still very youthful. Still very closed-in on the nose. A big, vigorous wine. Just beginning to come round now. The tannins are soft. The wine is full-bodied, voluptuous, rich, and intense. Very good acidity. It finishes much more stylishly than it starts. Very fine.
2005–28

Vintage 1994
This has a lovely perfumed nose. Medium body but stylish and balanced. Very lovely cool cassis fruit. Medium to medium-full body. The tannins are just about absorbed. Balanced. Surprisingly elegant and complex at the end. A splendid result for the vintage.
2005–08

Vintage 1993
A little fat and over-evolved, like the 1996. But lighter. This is a very pleasant wine. But it is a little one-dimensional. Medium body only. Decent length. Again a good result, especially for the vintage.
drink soon

Vintage 1992
The nose is quite mature now. Ripe, round, fresh, and fruity if only one-dimensional. A small wine. But quite pleasant. I prefer it to the 1993. It is fresher.
drink soon

Vintage 1990
Full colour. Just about mature. Very lovely, rich, complex, classy nose. Nicely cool. Very lovely fruit. Lots of depth and dimension here. Fullish body. Still quite sturdy. Very good grip. Not a bit rustic. Long. This is ready but will keep for ages. Really harmonious. Very fine plus.
2005–28

Vintage 1989
Good colour. Slightly tougher on the nose than the 1990. Ripe, rich, firm, and vigorous but not quite as rich and complete. I very much like the style here but it is more Syrah than Cabernet. More Rhône than Bordeaux. Very good grip. Long. Very fine again.
2005–20

Vintage 1988
Fine acidity. Very pure nose. Very elegant. Medium-full body. Very lovely fruit. Not as rich as the 1989 but, as in Hermitage, better balanced. Long, cool, complex, and very stylish. Fullish enough. Very fine plus.
2005–25

INDEX

Picture credits

top = t, bottom = b

Front cover: Tory McTernan; Alamy: Cephas Picture Library/Mick Rock: 49; Cephas Picture Library: Stephen Wolfenden 38, Ian Shaw 43, 44, Kjell Karlsson 122, Mick Rock 123, Nigel Blythe 133; Helge Hansen: 68, 71, 166 b, 167 b; Claes Löfgren/winepictures.com: 1, 2, 4, 8-9, 18, 30, 33, 35, 36, 40-41, 47, 56, 59, 60, 74, 76-77, 79, 80, 88, 90-91, 92, 93, 96, 97, 102, 105, 112, 114, 116-117, 119, 130-131, 139, 146, 156, 174, 177; Scope: Jean Luc Barde 140, 153 centre t, 153 centre b, 187, Jacques Guillard 50, 62, 63, 72, 108, 169; Jon Wyand: 158, 163, 164, 166 t, 167 t, 181, 182. Courtesy of the estates: 11, 12, 14, 15, deepix.com 17, 20, 21, 23, 24, 25, 26, 27, 29, 32, 46, 52, 53, 54, 57, 65, 66, 75, 82, 83, 84, 86, 87, 94, 98, 99, 100, 103, 106, 111, 113, 120, 125, 126, 128, 129, 122, 123, 136, 137, 142, 143, 145, 147, 148, 149, 151, 152, 153 t, 153 b, 154, 155, 159, 160, 161, 162, deepix.com 165, 168, 170, 171, 172, 173, 175, 176, 178, 179, 180, 183, 184, 185, 186, 188, 189